9 Months to say Goodbye

The Inspirational Story of

Virginia Rose

By: Jonathan Vandermark Jr.
(Virginia's Daddy)

Chapters:

Dedication: This book is dedicated to Virginia Rose Vandermark, whose grace, love, and joy changed the world.

Introduction

Through the pain there is love, in
the sorrow there is grace. With despair, joy
can be found. These are the lessons a 4-
year-old girl taught the world. That 4-year-
old girl is my Virginia Rose, or as Jenn says,
OUR Virginia Rose.

Do you remember the moment you
found out you were having a child? The
excitement, the nerves, the planning,
sharing the news with everyone... It would
take 9 months for that child to grow and
develop until one day, she would enter the
world.

As the father to a little boy full of life, not even a year-old yet, I can remember the moment my beautiful bride, Jenn, told me we were having another child. The overwhelming emotions, the waiting, and then the day we found out that our second child would be a girl. Oh my. My heart was so full. Before I even could hold her in my arms, she stole my heart.

There is something very special about the bond between a father and daughter. The same can be said of a mother and son. Something unique. Those nine months, waiting and planning, led up to an amazing February 1st. When my daughter, Virginia Rose, left the comfort and safety of her mother's womb and entered the safety of my arms. With tears flowing in the labor and delivery room, Virginia went to get her first check-up and tests. Perfect. 10 out of 10 on everything. She was a beautiful perfect baby girl.

My little Virginia Rose. Oh, how she captured my heart and the hearts of so many. Her infectious giggle. Her gorgeous smile. Her beautiful eyes would light up a room. She was a girly girl. Loved pink and purple, and anything princess. She was a Southern girl, with her gentile manners, and love of the garden and nature, and animals. She was feisty, would say what she was thinking, and was my beautiful little Southern Belle. In fact, we were in the process of moving to a farm in Charles City called Abundant Harvest Acres, something she was very excited about. RJ was going to oversee the chickens, and Virginia Rose wanted a cow named Annabelle, and a cat named Figaro. We were going to be filming a documentary in 2015, capturing the move and change to self-sustaining farm life.

Virginia Rose loved visiting with Grandma Boo and helping her in the garden. She always loved being outside. Eating some fresh grown produce that she and Grandma Boo planted, was the highlight of her trip. She was very excited to start our own farm and build her own little garden. Early in 2015, those plans were drastically changed.

I often think back on her life. The ups and the downs. I think back on my time as her father and the things she taught me that have made me a better dad to her brothers. The pain of losing her still hurts, and somedays waves of emotion can rip me apart, but time has begun to heal some wounds, and the clarity of how to live without her is much better.

We had nine months to welcome Virginia Rose and plan for her birth, God gave us another 9 months to say goodbye, as she slowly faded from my arms into Christs'.

This is her inspirational story. A story of grace, love, and joy. If you had 9-months to say goodbye, how would you?

April

With the beautiful warm spring sun shining down on us, we laughed and were filled with joy as we watched Virginia Rose collect Easter eggs. It was a weekend that would forever change our life. As we watched her play with her brothers and friends at Southside Church, we had no idea the storm that was brewing inside of her. We had no way to prepare for what the coming days would reveal.

Virginia Rose was a very joyous four-year-old princess. She loved everything pink and purple and adored fairy tale princesses. I can still see her in that gorgeous white Easter dress, frolicking around with the other children as they battled for all the brightly colored plastic eggs, filled with chocolate treasures. After she collected her prizes, we headed to MiMi and PaPa's home for Easter with the family.

She played on the trampoline with her cousins and showered us all with her smiles and laughter, our world was about to be completely turned upside down. As we enjoyed our family time, I often look back on those photos. I see things now, that I had no clue to look for then. Little bruises on her legs... a small rash on her arms... it would be her last Easter with us, and her last weekend on the trampoline with her cousins. It would be the last weekend her cousins would ever spend with her.

One of the cruelest realities of pediatric cancer is the often sudden "flip of the switch" it arrives as. Countless families have told us the same story repeatedly. A healthy child enjoying life is stricken ill and becomes feverish, maybe they have the flu. In our case, it was her rash.

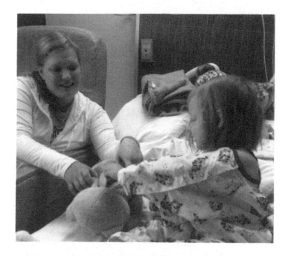

Virginia Rose loved to garden. She loved flowers and butterflies. She loved colors and painting. Easter weekend, before the egg hunt and trip to MiMi and PaPa's house, she was out in the yard planting flowers. It was just before the Easter egg hunt that we noticed her rash. Small red and purplish dots sprinkled around the bottom of her legs. Virginia had always had sensitive skin, so our initial thoughts were heat rash or a little bug bite from working in the sunshine. After all, the little spots were only where the sun touched her skin. We would later come to find out the "rash" we thought was a heat rash, was petechia from low platelets in her body.

As soon as we returned from MiMi and PaPa's for the weekend, we took Virginia to her doctor. The rash was spreading and seemed to get worse. In our minds, we thought it would be time to see a dermatologist, or do an allergy test, to see what was irritating her skin.

Jennifer took Virginia to the doctor and I stayed with the boys. I often think back on that morning. How normal it was for us. How ordinary and peaceful it was. So many times in our lives, isn't that when the storm hits? Just when you think you have something figured out... BAM! We were just a few weeks away from moving to our farm, putting the house on the market, making BIG changes... then the phone rang. It was Jenn. You know when your spouse calls and you can tell immediately by the cadence in their voice, by the pauses and inflections what is happening. Maybe a parental intuition that starts going off. This was one of those calls. As soon as Jenn started talking, I knew something was wrong.

She had been given the option to come home and pick me up or have an ambulance take the two of them to MCV. In our area, when the conversation finishes with MCV, all the flags are going off. There are fantastic hospitals closer, and if you are going to MCV, it is something usually extremely urgent or traumatic. As I started crying on the phone, I knew something bad was up, I told her to come home and please get me. I immediately called my father to see if he could sit with the boys. Just as PaPa always did, he rushed down to sit with them.

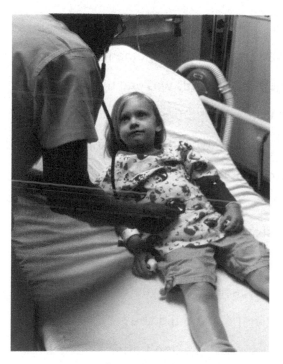

We took Virginia Rose to the emergency room at MCV, where they were expecting her. She was calm and patient as they ran some blood work. It did not take long for them to come back in her room and admit her.

Some moments in life leave you breathless and some moments take your breath away... this was one that did both to us. When we got upstairs to her room on the 7th floor, we were given more information. The initial labs painted a nasty picture. As we were taken into the hallway to talk with the doctor, we heard the words we all dread, cancer. Cancer? She was a healthy, active, fit, 4-year-old girl. Cancer? How in the world did she get cancer? We don't smoke. We don't drink. All these "how" questions started swirling... as I broke down crying in the hospital hallway that evening, I knew I had to remain strong for my baby girl.

Those first hours after diagnosis quickly turned into days. Time felt like it had stopped and there were a lot of logistical things to start figuring out. One of the hardest things after diagnosis was to notify family members. Who do you call, and how do you inform them? These are all very personal decisions that everyone needs to make very carefully. That evening, I called my father to give him the update. As I wept on the phone, the strength and comfort of his voice gave me the strength I needed. He took our boys back to Williamsburg with him while we got more answers and figured out what Virginia Rose was going to need.

Having no medical background, myself, those first days in April were extremely difficult and confusing. Even when advised not to research online, and find all the horror stories, I undoubtedly went right to Google to see what I could find. I read case studies, protocols, and experimental treatments. My head would spin trying to make sense of it all. As the parent, I needed to be informed, and needed to have all my questions answered, but what information did I need, and what questions should I ask? Her medical team was very willing to answer any questions I had. I am thankful for their openness and patience with me. As you might imagine, those first days and weeks were very emotional. Saying goodbye to Virginia Rose was nowhere close to a reality in our minds. She was strong, had a great team, we just needed to fight this thing. Right?

It was about two weeks after diagnosis that things took another turn, and saying goodbye started entering our minds.

Virginia Rose finished up her first round of chemo, a 10-day treatment, "induction" round. She tolerated it well and was not experiencing too many negative side effects. After her induction, we awaited results, results that were going to challenge us in new ways.

As we waited for all the results to come in, she began her 2nd round of chemo. This round would include some stronger drugs and would not be as long. Shortly after starting her 2nd round, all while being inpatient, the results were in. The blasts in her blood went from 51% to 50%, virtually no response to the chemo. In addition to this devastating news, her testing from two weeks ago came back from the lab in Seattle. It revealed she had monosomy 7. This was a mutation of her 7th chromosome, which made her a high-risk case. This was not something we were even looking for in the test results or expecting. An extremely rare mutation, it painted a grim prognosis. April seemed to go from bad to worse almost daily as more lab results came in. By the end of the month, she failed two rounds of chemo, making her refractory, and had this monosomy-7 issue to complicate her treatment. We began looking at other treatment options for her, including St. Jude Children's Research Hospital in Tennessee.

In just one month, our beautiful 4-year-old princess went from playing outside in the beautiful Spring weather with friends and family to living in the hospital literally fighting for her life. April was our first month to say goodbye. Just like a pregnancy, that first month revealed symptoms, lab work, and results. As I wept in the hospital room, cleaned up after Virginia would get sick, took a crash course in medical terminology, prayed with tears, and sweat pouring from my face, the reality of her situation reached our community. We began to see God do amazing things in people's lives, and our little girls' story was only beginning… God was just getting started.

May

After that first month, a month of bad news on top of bad news sandwiched in-between bad news... we started to anticipate the symptoms better. Just like the second month of pregnancy, we were getting into the rhythm of this new life. The doctor's rounds, lab results, protocols... but there were also physical changes happening. Virginia had now lost her hair, and the cancer and drugs were starting to take a physical toll on her little body.

Virginia Rose developed a fungal infection while at MCV. An infection that was a known side effect of the cancer and drugs. As her body was weak from the cancer and chemo, and her immune system was completely offline for a whole month, simple viruses that she could normally fight became deadly. She had developed a persistent fever, cough, and shortness of breath. No matter what her medical team tried, it just wouldn't help.

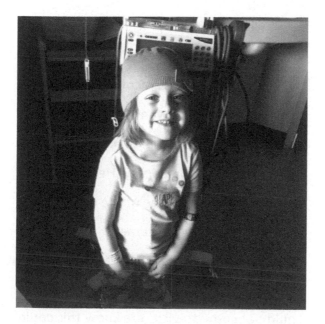

By May we were in contact with St. Jude, and we were exploring treatment options for her there. Unfortunately, this issue needed to be addressed first. Solving this infection she developed, became the new priority, as any treatment for her cancer had to be put on hold.

Those long days were filled with visits from friends and family early on, but as the reality and fragility of her condition became clearer, she went into quarantine. We had to limit the volume and length of visits quickly and drastically. Her fun time with Child Life and some of the other kids on the 7th floor had to come to a stop. She could not go out and visit with her new friends, and her friends outside the hospital could not come to visit. We knew this could take a huge mental toll on her, so Jenn and I did all we could to keep her engaged and active. MCV did a great job sending volunteers and teachers to come work with her one-on-one. She was even able to still see Aunt Sarah, as she worked just a few floors up at MCV and was able to visit and play with Virginia Rose. Virginia loved her Aunt Sarah, and all of the fun they had together. Having her just a call away two floors up, was a huge blessing.

Her hospital room, going on two months now, was all decorated with cards and art from friends, and she had a huge window looking out onto the 7th floor playground. This was a fantastic thing for her, as it allowed us to monitor the area, and she could go outside to the playground for a private session when it was empty.

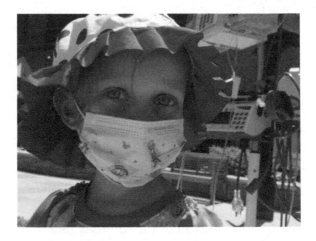

I remember the joy she had when we would go outside and play. Those trips were limited to family only with her by this point, but she had so much fun playing hide and seek out there. She would look off over the city and say, "hey dad look, it's my city". She loved life and was full of so much joy. I knew we would do everything we could to fight this cancer, but would it be enough?

How in the world were we going to stop this infection? What was causing this infection?

By the end of April, the thought that she may not survive this cancer began to creep into my mind. I remember hating myself for even thinking it. I felt like a horrible dad for even entertaining that notion. As we went into May I began having bad nightmares about losing her. I would wake up almost every hour to check on her. I can still hear the beep, beep, beep, of her IV machine sometimes.

As we went through May, her medical team decided we needed to go in and drain fluid from her left lung. With her fever and breathing getting worse, and medicine not helping, they wanted to go in.

We knew that unless we got some answers on her infection, she would not be able to go to St. Jude.

By this time, Virginia Rose had been under anesthesia for her marrow aspirates a few times and was getting used to going down for procedures. She had her favorite stuffed animals with her, and a beautiful pillowcase hand-made by a dear friend. As we prayed with her and she fell asleep, we waited as we always did in the waiting area. This time, it was different.

They came and told us they were having a hard time waking her up, and that her breathing and blood pressure dropped. She was being transferred to the pediatric intensive care, which was on the 7th floor as well, just on the other side of the hallway. They let us back to see her in the recovery area, as they were still waking her and monitoring her vitals with a dedicated nurse. As she woke and her numbers began to recover, we were headed to her room.

Her doctor explained to us what happened. What they had thought was fluid buildup in her lungs was actually dead tissue. Her infection was necrotic and was killing her lung. There was nothing for them to drain, and the procedure caused her frail body to panic and crash.

Although we now had an answer and clarity to her lung issue, we were left wondering what that would mean for further treatment here or with St. Jude.

I remember settling into her new room. In fact, as we looked out the window it was directly across from her other room. You could see the playground from her window, and you could see all her art in her other room's window. If she needed to stay more than 24 hours in the ICU, we would have to pack up her other room. Thankfully, she bounced back and the next day we were back in her regular room and out of the ICU. The question of her treatment and the urgency of a plan was now more pressing than ever. It was time to act.

I remember Jenn and I meeting with her medical team and speaking with St. Jude. We were now just waiting for the final word from them. Her updated status with her lung was sent to them for consideration, and we were awaiting the yes or no. It had been almost a month since she had had any chemo, or treatment for her cancer now. She had spent the month of May battling this infection in quarantine and getting blood and platelet transfusions weekly.

Our second month to say goodbye was filled with a lot of fight. We were not giving up, and the enemy was trying to break us and beat us down, but when the dust settled, God was going to see a victory in Virginia Rose.

We got the call back from St. Jude and they accepted her as a patient. They were going to send a med-flight to pick her and Jenn up. What a blessing. It was the hope that we were desperately praying for. Just a chance. Just a glimmer of hope that my little girl would have a chance to beat this. That week we got ready. We had a prayer service at Parkway Baptist, where my old high school buddy, Mike, led us in prayer for Virginia Rose and travel. In those first two months, we saw God showing up in so many ways. We call them angels in disguise.

Angels in sheriffs' uniforms who showed up to hold a carwash to raise money for Virginia Rose.
Angels who would send prayers and cards to her at MCV.
Angels who were on the 7th floor with Virginia Rose battling cancer too, who loved

on her and helped her more than they
knew.

Angels who would come every day to take
her vitals and help her with her
medications.

Angels who would stay past their shift to
pray with us.

Angels wearing nurse uniforms.

By the end of May, our second
month to say goodbye, we were filled with
hope and thankfulness as we got ready to
head to Memphis.

June

The third month in pregnancy we know is the end of the first trimester. It was really a HUGE transition for us as we headed to St. Jude. Leaving our support network, friends, and family was a big decision, but we knew that if there was a place and team that could help our little girl, it was there.

They came with a med-flight to pick up Jenn and Virginia Rose. I remember flying out that morning on a stand-by ticket I was able to get, thanks to Parkway Baptist. I left Richmond around 5 AM and arrived in Memphis before they did. Jenn has some videos and photos of their trip, and I am so amazed when I watch them. The gentleness and care they gave my girls make me tear up just writing about it. My little girl was so weak and tired from the trip but was ready for her new hospital adventure. She even had her favorite stuffed bear right there with her on the plane.

I was at St. Jude when they arrived. My heart was racing when I saw the ambulance pull up. Because Virginia Rose was a medical transport from another hospital, she was in quarantine upon arrival. They had a little tent that covered her in her bed as she was taken to the Leukemia ward. It was night and day from MCV, which I would expect. I remember getting into her new room and meeting her new medical team. Her first day, in that first week of

June, was filled with tests, bloodwork, and scans. They had all the notes from MCV but obviously needed to get their baseline for her treatment.

The treatment we went for was going to take cells from me, and/or Jenn and use those to try and help her system fight the cancer. We already knew the standard treatment was not working and the monosomy-7 was making things worse for her. On top of that, we knew that her fungal infection had caused her left lung to decay, and her fevers were still persistent. Even with all of that, we still had hope... for now.

We were only there a day when we had a meeting with her medical team. It seemed that there was something else happening, we were unaware of. Another storm that was brewing undetected inside of little Virginia Rose.

When she was diagnosed with cancer and went through all the tests and procedures at MCV, she was given repeated echocardiograms to monitor her heart. I remember the first one she had. In fact, we have it all on video. The technician had her cart by Virginia's bed and applied the "belly jelly" as Virginia referred to it. Virginia Rose looked up astonished and proclaimed, "I'm not having a baby". Even in the most stressful moments, Virginia could make us laugh.

I am often reminded of that moment. When stress seems to build up in my life. When work gets really hard and the world seems like it is crashing down, I think of Virginia Rose in that hospital bed. I think of her sweet spirit filled with joy, and I remember to take a deep breath and keep putting one foot in front of the other.

As we met with her new medical team they asked if she had any heart issues. It was not a question we were anticipating, but it was one I was prepared for.

I kept a binder full of all her notes and lab results, so I was able to quickly reference her past echoes. They did not show any issues.

Her new team proceeded to inform us that her ejection fraction and shorting fraction were off. This was a major concern, and they would need to move her to the ICU at St. Jude.

We had only been there a day, and this reality was not what we had in our mind. All our hopes, all of the anticipation and work to get here, and now her heart is failing. How can this be?

What we have since learned is that the strong chemo drugs used can cause heart damage. It is normally seen years after treatment, but in her case, as with everything it seemed, she was the exception to the rule.

We moved over to the ICU. I remember PaPa carrying her the whole way down the halls. It was not really that much to move, as we just got there. They sent over cardiac support from Le Bonheur Children's Hospital just down the road and began treating her heart failure. The next day everything changed again…

It was during the rounds that the ICU doctor informed my father and I of the situation. Obviously, St. Jude is a cancer hospital, and with Virginia's heart condition now, they cannot treat her cancer. We would have the option to transfer to Le Bonheur to address her heart failure and come back when it was fixed, or we may want to head home and be with family. They were not aware of the severity of her heart condition when they accepted her as a patient, and had they known, they would not have brought her here.

Needless to say, I was devastated. After everything, we finally are here, and now we have to leave without any treatment for her cancer. Now, we have to battle heart failure.

About 30-minutes later the doctor returned. My father and I had not told Jenn yet. She was downstairs with MiMi and the boys. He told us there was a change of plans from what he just said. After a conversation, with a team much higher than him he said, they decided to keep Virginia Rose another night and re-evaluate in the morning. Something would have to change though. Between her refractory cancer, monosomy-7, fevers from the fungal infection, and now heart failure... no one would touch her.

That night, she was so weak. We thought we might be coming to an end. We gathered around her ICU bed and prayed. We gave her a music box we were saving for her, and a little smile broke through. It was over... hope was all but gone... but for God.

Friends, I know that Virginia Rose's life story is one that evokes many emotions. Even now as I write and think about everything she went through; I have to take breaks to "cry it out". When I think of everything she endured and how quickly her life changed, it leaves me speechless. I can tell you with 100% certainty, the doctors thought she was done, when we looked at her and her labored breathing and fevers, we thought this was the end, with her heart failing, everything pointed to the end.

I have a paper in my binder from the next day. It is a graph of her vitals charted out. That next morning, after two months of constant fevers from her fungal infection, her fever broke. With no new treatment.

With no change in diet. With all hope
fading, that fever just went away. Not only
did it go away, but it never came back at all.
I am here to tell you that we were
witnessing God work a miracle in our little
girl.

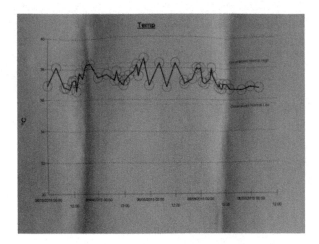

As her new medical team came by,
they agreed to keep her another day. She
was on a day-to-day basis, and they needed
to see changes for her to stay. The next day

she was doing even better. Her color started coming back. Her red blood count was coming back, her ANC was coming back... the next day, without any treatments, she was at levels prior to when she was admitted to the ER on April 7th. That ICU room was becoming a place of miracles. I have two videos of her in that room that I love to watch together. One is when she was almost gone and we gave her the ballerina music box, the other is a few days later when she is giggling and playing in her blanket in the ICU bed.

The conversations with her medical team now changed to treatment options again. With her fevers gone and her body healing, we could now tackle this left lung. They would need to do surgery and remove it. Obviously, any lung surgery will have major risks, but with her fragility and cancer, they were elevated. I remember her surgeon, a UVA man (of course), going through the plan with us. He was going to go in on a Friday and remove the dead tissue, the lower lobe of her left lung. He would have her intubated and we agreed with nutrition to put a feeding line in. She should be sedated, he told us, through the weekend, and on Monday would start recovery. He was helping us understand the dangers of the surgery and how different she would look after. We understood and prepared for a long weekend. I remember when they gave Virginia the knockout juice. She was in PaPa's arms in the prep area, and she started getting silly. PaPa gently laid her in the bed, and they wheeled her

back, with Jenn by her side. As we prayed
and sent Virginia Rose back, we began to
wait.

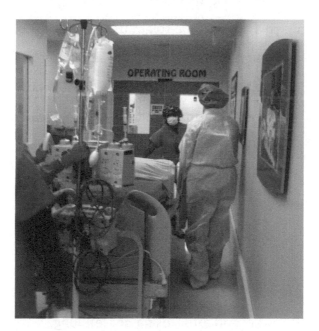

If you are a parent and have waited
for your child during surgery, you know the
feeling as you wait on news, any news. As

the minute hand ticked, we waited. As the hour hand moved, we waited.

Jenn and I were in her ICU room when a nurse came to get us. It seems like it takes an hour for them to speak when it probably took 2 seconds, but she could not speak quickly enough. She asked if we were Virginia's parents, we proudly said yes. She informed us the surgery was complete and she was asking for daddy.

Asking for daddy? How can that be? She was going to be sedated and intubated this weekend after losing her left lung. When we arrived in the recovery area of the ICU there she was in her bed. As she heard us and saw me, she tried to sit up and grab a hold of me. I will forever cherish that hug.

Friends, that was a miracle hug. I have a photo from that moment. Her team informed us they had her intubated for the surgery and she did great. They took that out and had her on oxygen. She was breathing so well; they took her off oxygen and she was now on room air. ROOM AIR! Just after losing half of her left lung. The little girl who was coughing and feverish for two months... the little girl who was having heart failure... my little Virginia Rose!! God did a miracle that day. He used the team at St. Jude to save Virginia Rose when everyone thought she was done.

When I say everyone thought she was done, this is why... when you become a patient at St. Jude, they schedule one of the photographers to take photos and they do a

welcome process with the social workers.
We were there that whole time leading up
and had no visit. We never got the
photographer to come and do her photos...
they wrote her off as soon as she arrived.

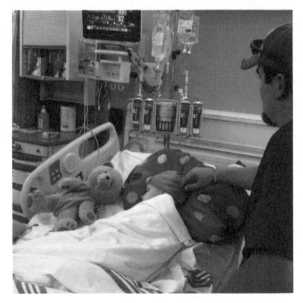

Sometimes in life, we can feel that
way. Friend, you may be reading this little
book on Virginia Rose's battle, and you
might feel like the whole world has written
you off. You may feel like your family has

written you off. You may feel like your spouse has written you off. You may feel like your doctors have written you off, but I am here to tell you that GOD has not written you off. He will come through and HE will do what only He can do. We are confident that Virginia Rose's time on this earth was coming to an end, and to be honest, we were not ready for that. Not that you are ever ready to see your child die, but we were in a real rough spot. Just when we had hope, it was dashed, and if we lost Virginia Rose that first week of June... I just don't know... but God knows. HE knew what was about to happen.

That next week Virginia Rose began healing up from her surgery. We had our meeting with the social worker. We got our orientation. We never did get the photos though, but she did make it in one of the St. Jude commercials for Thanksgiving that year.

With her body healing up, we could now get back on a treatment plan. Jenn and I went and had our lab work done, so we could start the process of this new trial drug. By Jenn's birthday, June 19th, Virginia Rose was able to leave her hospital room and go to the Tri Delta House, which is a hotel on campus. It would be her first non-medical trip outside the hospital since April 7th.

St. Jude is an amazing place where the children don't have to stay inpatient like they would at a traditional hospital. With the on and off-campus housing, the kids can leave the hospital rooms and be with their families. What a blessing that was to leave the hospital with her. Of course, that was also the weekend her favorite movie would come out, "Inside Out".

St. Jude gave her a little backpack with a portable IV for her medicines, and Jenn was trained on how to give her meds through it and how to do her bandage changes with her port. With this new freedom, St. Jude style, she was able to go to the movie theatre to see "Inside Out" on June 21st.

She was so excited to be out, off-campus, and at a movie theater. I remember holding her hand as we walked to the ticket booth. She was jumping up and down, and sure enough, she fell. My heart sank. All this time and she fell. She scraped her knee, but not bad. We got her a band-aid from the staff and she was good to go. Determined to watch her movie with a big bucket of fresh popcorn.

Virginia rose would remember that fall she had and would use it to scare me time and time again over the coming months. She knew how to get her daddy, and that one would get me good.

After that, she enjoyed taking her first trip to the Memphis Zoo. She absolutely loved animals, and this place had them all for her. She was particularly fond of the big polar bear. She would love to watch him swim in the water and would just giggle as he played. Capping off her hot trip to the zoo, she enjoyed a big ice cream cone.

By the end of June, we were settling into our new life in Memphis at St. Jude. With her fungal infection gone, her dead lung tissue gone, we now focused on her heart treatment and cancer treatment. The heart treatment would be done at Le Bonheur and her cancer treatment would be done at St. Jude. Her youngest brother Samuel was a perfect 10-for-10 match for a BMT (Bone Marrow Transplant), so he was coming to stay with us in Memphis while RJ, her older brother, would stay in Virginia with MiMi and PaPa. Housing was only provided for 4 people, so RJ needed to stay back in Virginia.

We had her BMT meeting on June 29th and went over the process and expectations. Of course, the greatest concern was her heart failure. We would need to get that under control and at a manageable level before they would start a BMT process on her. On this big day, with all my nerves in a bunch, she did what only she could do… she would once again make daddy laugh. After her echo for that day, she decided to take a nice little stroll down the hallway. Of course, skipping and jumping… making me nervous with every bounce, giggling at my reaction every time.

After her BMT appointment, we started getting ready to move into a more permeant location with St. Jude. We would be transferring to their long-term housing, Target House.

Just as the third month marks the end of the first trimester, the end of June marked the end of a big chapter in Virginia Rose's journey and started a new one. We were now living in miracle over time with her, and the habit of making memories every chance we could get had begun.

July

By July we were making memories with Virginia Rose every chance we could get. Our new little apartment was right near the Memphis Zoo, and she loved visiting there. On top of that, PaPa was about to be back with Sam. He was needed as we started the BMT process, and PaPa was dropping off a vehicle for us so we could get Virginia Rose around town without renting cars.

After her morning appointments in "A Clinic", we were playing in the leukemia wing when we saw PaPa's truck pull in at the hospital. Virginia Rose giggled, and we hurried down to meet them. She hadn't seen Sam or PaPa since her surgery and had so much to tell them. She had to show them her new apartment too.

There are no adequate words to describe the love Virginia Rose and PaPa had for each other. Their bond was beyond special. She absolutely adored her PaPa, and he absolutely cherished her. Seeing them together was something truly special to behold.

She quickly had to show PaPa all her new adventures. This was the first time he had seen her out of the hospital since he came to watch the boys on April 7th. She paraded him around, giving him a grand tour of her new hospital. Then she took him to her new apartment and gave him the VIP treatment. Of course, she had to take him to her new zoo and see her polar bear friend.

Those days were some of the best days we had in Memphis. Her summer treatment was to make memories, enjoy the sunshine, and get that heart ready for a BMT. Boy did we make some memories. Now with Sam moving in with us, Virginia had a little partner to play with 24/7...

At the end of that week, it was time for PaPa to head back home. He was leaving his old truck with us to use around town and was flying back home. Virginia Rose had an appointment at Le Bonheur that day. She was excited to show him her other hospital, her heart hospital.

There are some difficult goodbyes in life. Times when you want more than anything to stay, but you must go. This was that day for PaPa. It was an emotional goodbye, as he hugged Virginia Rose and headed to the airport. We had a rule for the family during Virginia Rose's fight. As much as possible, don't cry in front of her. We all would get emotional, but we all tried to step out of the room quietly when we felt the overwhelming emotion coming. We wanted nothing but hope for her. That was one of the hardest moments to hold in the tears. I know PaPa wanted to stay, and Virginia wanted him to stay.

Virginia Rose loved her heart hospital and had fun listening to her "heart bark", as she would say. With her treatment for the summer, she was seeing results, and with support, her heart was getting stronger again. She was even able to take Sam to a baseball game. They had so much fun eating popcorn and hanging out at the park.

With Sam now with us, he had to have his labs drawn too. Let's just say he was not a fan. We called him super Sam with supercells. They drew up his labs and confirmed he had the matching cells for her BMT, now we just needed to wait.

Just like that second trimester, the 4th month to say goodbye saw many of the symptoms and side effects going away from the first trimester, and we set into a solid routine for this new life. We were now in a

season of waiting. Waiting for the date for
her BMT and passing the summer days
making memories.

August

Now in the 5th month, it was time to let Virginia Rose express herself. Just like a baby starting to stretch and kick in her mom's belly, Virginia Rose was ready to make a big impact.

During her treatment at MCV and even as she transitioned to St. Jude, Virginia Rose was blessed to have so many prayer warriors, angels in disguise, and friends who loved on her and us. Simple cards in the mail, gift cards for special treats, money to help with bills, gifts for her to stay busy, and notes of encouragement filled her mailbox. Virginia Rose was ready to give back.

Childhood cancer impacts so many families every year. It does not care who you are or where you come from. It does not discriminate on your skin color, it does not care about your gender, it pays no attention to your age, and could care less what's in your bank account. Many families are hit with unexpected news and are thrust into a whole new world.

We were incredibly blessed to have such an amazing support team to encourage us and help us in the fight. Virginia Rose wanted to help other kids she had met and even ones she had not met, in their fight. In August, she began sending out what she called Boxes of Love.

These boxes were filled with toys and crafts to keep a child busy in the hospital during treatments, or while at home recovering. In addition to the gifts, each box had a note of encouragement and a gift card for gas and/or groceries. Virginia Rose wanted to give back and help other kids.

I remember her writing the little cards and taking them down to the mailbox at the Target House to mail out. She even had a pink wagon she would load the boxes onto to take to the post office and mail out.

One of the greatest questions faced in Virginia's journey was, what would you do if you only had a short time left to live. If the realization that we are not guaranteed tomorrow sits in, and if we thought about what we would do if we didn't have much time on earth left, what would we do?

Many of us might think about that bucket list of things to do. We might have a list of places to go, people to see, experiences, and alike. I know that for Virginia Rose, I had a list of things, memories, I wanted to make with her. There were things I wanted her to experience, and things I was going to work hard to make sure she would get to do. As her father, I wanted all those things for her... but she reminded me that in life's ending moments, when we have a short time to say goodbye, it's not about the things we get to experience, it's about the people we get to impact. The story of Virginia Rose is that in her last months of life, she wanted to serve others. In her final moments, she wanted to love others.

I remember when PaPa came and donated blood and platelets, he came back to the room and Virginia Rose was very concerned for him. She held his hand and checked his bandage. She was concerned with him, had compassion for him, empathy for what he was experiencing. That was who she was.

In Virginia Rose's final months on this earth, with just 9-months to say goodbye, she impacted lives all around the world. She decided to serve others and love others. Her boxes were filled with things to help someone's day, but more importantly, she filled them with love and compassion.

Maybe that is a lesson we all can learn from Virginia Rose, and it is one that we learn from Jesus in the Bible. It is in His final moments, when He knows death is coming, how did he spend His final moments? Loving others, and washing feet...

August was a hard month, as we awaited Virginia's lab results and prayed daily for her BMT. It was in the waiting, knowing if she couldn't get the BMT, knowing if her heart didn't recover, we were saying goodbye to her, that she showed us what to do in our final moments, and reminded us all of the impact one life can have on others.

As I look back on the nine months I had to say goodbye to my little girl, I am thankful for August. A month of waiting for answers, and a month of seeing the true meaning in living like we are dying.

September

Month number 6 was one of the hardest for me. The end of the 2nd trimester, the end is approaching. For us, it was a reality that we didn't want to hear or accept.

When hope fades, darkness wants to come and steal the day. I know that September was that moment. After three months of getting Virginia Rose ready for her BMT, we had the meeting with her team. Her summer numbers were looking good, but the cancer was strengthening. After her strong recovery and miracle healing in June, her body was starting to go through blood products quickly again. Her heart made great progress, but her cancer was progressing too.

I had a meeting set with her team that second week of September. Here are my posts those days:

Sept 7: *Tomorrow Virginia will most likely get her 27th blood transfusion. She was at 8.8 on Friday, so we will see (she gets a transfusion when it gets at or below 8.0).*

September is Childhood Cancer Awareness month; you may have seen her new foundation. Thank you so much for helping make that possible. Here is another great way to help children fighting cancer like Virginia Rose. Give Blood and Platelets.

Virginia has had 26 going on 27 blood transfusions in the last 5 months.

__Sept. 8__: Please pray for us and the BMT team. They will meet tomorrow to decide, and we are asking the Lord to open this door.

Her numbers today confirm the AML is coming back again...

She is getting her 27th blood transfusion today, expected, but not expected is a platelet transfusion. She tore through her transfusion on Friday, and once again there are blasts in her blood, 12%.

There is an urgency in our spirit this time, and we are asking for you all to pray for this

BMT to start. She has done everything, and more, that St. Jude has asked her to do to get ready. If they say no tomorrow, not sure what we will do.

Her AML has stayed quiet for 2 months, and it has been a great two months to let her enjoy life and let her heart recover, and it has. Now it looks like this horrendous AML is strengthening again, and the stronger it gets the harder a successful BMT will be. This last week we kept seeing little signs that the AML was strengthening again, and it has.

Her numbers today - Platelet 10, Hemoglobin 7.1, WBC 1.1, ANC 100, Blasts 12%

With ANC still at 100, she still cannot go to the zoo or parks. ☐

Please pray.

Sept. 9: *No news today. We will find out tomorrow. Her labs are at 10:30 and she sees her Dr. at 12:15. It will be a long night, with a lot on our minds. Virginia Rose had fun with PaPa John today. We are curious to what her numbers will be tomorrow after the double transfusion yesterday.*

Sept. 10: *Heading over to St. Jude Children's Research Hospital - Please pray for peace for whatever happens today. It will probably be around 1 (2EST) for the word. Thank you for your prayers.*

Sept 14: *Please join with us in prayer today at 2:30C/3:30Est. We have our meeting at 3PM/(4 East) and are calling on prayer warriors to flood heaven at 2:30. Please pray for calm, peace, strength, and patience in today's meeting. Please pray for the Lord to show us HIS path forward and grant us wisdom and discernment. Thank you all so much!*

Those days were filled with much anxiety as we awaited the news. Ultimately, September was the month that the options were all used up. I sat with her team, the whole team, and her social worker, as they explained her case and their decision. Because of her refractory AML, with monosomy 7, because of her heart failure and the infection issues, they decided unanimously that she would not be able to do a BMT, nor could they do any more treatments on her weak heart. If she was facing one of those issues, they would take the risk, but with all of them combined they said it would be malpractice to do the BMT.

It was incredibly difficult news to hear. The hope of Sam being her BMT was off the table. Her medical team gave her 3-12 months to live. Because of this, they reached out to her Make-A-Wish team in Virginia and were able to help get it expedited from December to October. We were very grateful for their hard work in that, but still wrestling with the news.

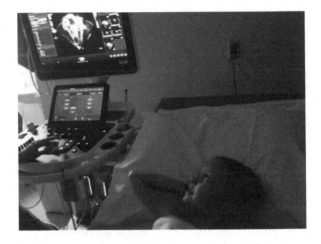

It was a difficult few days, to say the least. In the moment we felt misled, that the BMT was never really an option, that false hope was given. The enemy wanted to get in and disrupt those last months we would have with Virginia Rose. We resolved not to let that happen. We would remain in hope. We would remain thankful for these extra months we had with her. We would be forever grateful for the miracle that happened in June to bring us to this moment.

It was then I truly realized the meaning of Scripture reminding us of the work God has done in the past. I wanted to sit in the sadness of the moment, forgetting the work He had done to get us to this point. That is us in life so many times. We get into a difficult and broken situation, and instead of seeing how God has delivered us and carried us, we get bogged down in that moment and want to throw it all away.

We resolved to not let the enemy have a victory here, and we would praise God for all He had done in getting us this far. He had provided in so many ways and His angels in disguise were with us every step of the way.

Remaining confident in prayer for Virginia Rose's healing, we set out to make these final months filled with loving Virginia Rose and others.

Now that Sam would not be needed for the BMT, I took him back home and picked up RJ. We wanted him to have some memories and a great time exploring Virginia's new hospital too.

Virginia Rose was so excited to have her big brother back. They were two peas in a pod and best friends. She showed him all the exciting things on campus and took him to all her favorite places.

St. Jude was amazing to let us stay if we would like, and Virginia Rose would still get all her blood products and heart support. We decided to stay until the end of October, after her Make-A-Wish, and then would head back to Virginia.

September was a difficult month for sure and was filled with so many emotions. Through all the incredible ups and downs, Virginia Rose remained joyful and continued sending out her boxes to other kids fighting.

With the months left to say goodbye counting down, we made it a renewed priority to spread love and joy, just as Virginia Rose taught us.

October

Month 7 seemed to come quickly, as the countdown to Virginia Rose's big trip was in full swing. Back in April when she was diagnosed with AML, Make-A-Wish came and asked her to make a wish.

Let's just say that Virginia Rose was something of a princess-loving Southern belle. She loved Rapunzel, Cinderella, Belle, Aurora, Anna, and of course her new favorite, Joy. So, it didn't take long for her to let them know she wanted to see the princesses for Christmas at Disney.

With the trip expedited due to her updated prognosis, they did an amazing job getting her all set for an amazing visit.

From the flight to Disney to the return, it was a magical adventure. I remember when we arrived, and she got into her little villa. She was so excited and immediately went to put on all her princess dresses. That quickly broke out into a little dance party in the living room.

Seeing the joy on her face as she danced with PaPa, hearing the giggles as he twirled her around will forever be a memory I cherish.

Virginia Rose was able to see all her favorite characters, enjoyed amazing VIP treatment throughout the park, and was even able to spend an awesome day with the dolphins at SeaWorld.

One of the greatest moments from the trip was her meeting, Cinderella. She was speechless as she went up to her and after her hug, she skipped all of the way back to us. She was beaming with excitement.

I look back on that week with so many amazing memories. Knowing that if God had not stepped in and worked the miracle He did in her back in June, none of this would have been possible.

After an amazing trip, we returned to St. Jude. As we began packing up her apartment, we started planning her return home.

During our time in Memphis, our local community rallied and loved on us. They began getting our home ready. With new windows donated for the house from Window World, a new roof from Southside Church, neighbors, friends, and family cleaning up and setting up her room and yard for her return, when we got word that the house was ready, we began the trip back home.

It is in moments like these that there are opportunities all around us to be love to one another. We experienced that firsthand, as people loved on Virginia Rose and our family.

Just like that 7th month when expecting, the nesting phase, getting everything set-up for the arrival of the baby kicks in, Virginia Rose's room was getting all set up for her arrival.

November

I was waiting at the airport, with a local news crew and family when they landed. Virginia Rose was home. It was a bittersweet homecoming for sure. We were so glad to be reunited back home as a family, but we knew that meant her cancer was still raging.

We quickly got settled back home, and Virginia Rose was so excited to see her new room and all her welcome home decorations. It was so special and so great to be back in our community surrounded by her support team again.

St. Jude would mail her medical supplies as she needed them, and MCV was taking care of her blood transfusions as she needed them. We were blessed to have home care from Noah's Children care for Virginia Rose in the comfort of her home. It was great to be back home.

It was in November that the St. Jude commercial with her started to air as well.

We saw her on TV a few times, and even in the movie theater. Just like that 8th month of pregnancy, the 8th month saying goodbye brought some of those Braxton Hicks contractions. Virginia Rose would have moments for sure, and it was different not being at St. Jude for her care anymore. We kept seeing little signs of the cancer growing, and the helpless feeling there was nothing we could do about it.

In our minds, when her team said 3-12 months, we naturally thought, ok we have a year with her... we never thought it would be the lower end. It was becoming obvious though, the lower end was reality.

Her medical team was going over her blood transfusions, and by their calculation on how quickly she was going through them, felt she may not make it to Christmas. We began having discussions on how Christmas would look for her, and how to proceed with family and friends.

After talking with her medical team and realizing how quickly she would be fading, we decided to have Christmas with her every weekend. The little girl who gave us all so much. The one who would send out gifts to other kids fighting was about to have a huge party.

Starting in November, churches, friends, family, neighbors, organizations, and strangers all came together to throw her Christmas parties every week. Even as her body was getting weaker, she was so excited when they would show up. She even had a fun party planned for her big brother, RJ's 6th birthday.

Virginia Rose loved to plan parties. All the little details, all of the food, all of the music... every little part, she was a party planner.

It was so much fun to see her enjoying life. She planted some flowers with MiMi in the yard. She spent a few days on the trampoline with her brothers. She was able to even get a real dog named Rose Bud.

I am reminded of my journal post from **November 19th**: *Virginia Rose had a long night of sleep, and got up a little after 11 this morning. It amazes me to see her joy in the exhaustion. Between Rosebud and Legos, she is so grateful and happy. I just want to hold her and fix her. Thank you all for loving on Virginia Rose and my family. Even though her body is failing her, the Lord never will, and continues to give her* *strength through this enormous storm for such a little girl. We love you sweetie.*

Maybe you have been in those moments when exhaustion and brokenness surround you. I want you to be encouraged to find joy, joy even during the pain. Even in the storms and brokenness, you can find hope and joy. Just like Virginia Rose did. Joy in Jesus.

December

That final month. The last leg of the journey. I remember when Virginia Rose was born. That February morning, filled with all the anticipation and excitement to finally hold my baby girl. How special that day was.

I remember Jenn being ready for her to come out. As the days went on that January, you knew she was going to exit mommy's tummy any day. Just like that January in 2011, December 2015 was filled with expecting days. We knew, with every passing day, her time with us on earth was coming to an end. We were in the final month, the final moments with our Virginia

Rose. With one last month, how would we say goodbye?

Virginia Rose loved Christmas. I mean, loved, loved, loved Christmas. You might think, yeah, what kid doesn't like presents... but it was not that part, it was all the decorating. She was the party planner and throwing Jesus a birthday party was a highlight of her year. She would decorate cookies, build gingerbread houses. She would buy gifts for her brothers and wrap them with tender care. Then came the house decorations.

Before we left St. Jude, Virginia Rose went to the little gift shop. She would always like to stop and see what stuffed animals they would have. She acquired quite a collection over the months living there, but this time she was on a different mission. She was on the hunt for Christmas decorations. As she looked over the treasures in the shop, she fell in love with the ornaments. One by one she looked them over, each one better than the last. She just had to have them for her tree at home. We collected the ones she found, and then she found ones for all her grandparents to take back home for Christmas. This girl LOVED everything about Christmas.

One of the unfortunate things about her time at St. Jude, as I mentioned before, was that she did not get to experience all the photos that can go along with being a patient there. She was excited to be in the Thanksgiving commercial but was sad to miss out on the photos. In fact, she was scheduled to be in the 2015 Christmas catalog. The ALSAC photography crew had made an appointment with her to come over to the Target House and do a Christmas photoshoot. They were going to bring her over outfits to model and take her photo opening presents. Of course, Virginia Rose was very excited about that. The morning of her big photoshoot arrived, and she got all ready with mommy. Unfortunately, though, ALSAC had an unexpected power outage that morning and threw everything off. Virginia Rose never did get to do the Christmas photoshoot.

Sometimes life can just keep throwing those punches at you. Maybe you have been in a similar situation when expectations fall short, or you get all ready for something and then it never happens. It was amazing to watch her bounce right back from that disappointment and carry on with her day. I still remember the frustration and sadness of that moment, but my Virginia Rose didn't let it stick with her.

We still collect the St. Jude Christmas ornaments every year. Virginia's little tree can no longer hold them all, so we built a little St. Jude Christmas Forest with little trees all adorned with the St. Jude ornaments. It is a special way to remember her every Christmas and to continue in her awe and joy seeing all the new ornaments every year.

As Virginia Rose weakened throughout December, her community continued to rally around her. One evening our neighborhood showed up in the front yard with a parade, gifts, and caroling outside her windows. I held her in my arms, wrapped her in a blanket, and went onto the front porch to listen and see all her friends. She was so tired and so weak but loved seeing her friends.

One special Christmas party was when PaPa John and Nanny Gail came over with a very special surprise. After a knock on the door, Virginia Rose put on her beautiful winter coat and stepped outside into a winter wonderland. PaPa John had bought her a snow machine, and as the snowflakes fell she reached out to grab them. One of my favorite photos from her Christmas parties, was her outstretched arms, in her winter jacket, grabbing the snow from the sky.

She still had her appointments at MCV and was getting her meds and blood transfusions. Each visit's labs painted a picture of the end. She was no longer holding blood products, as her marrow was slowly dying. Her body was not making much anymore, and she was increasingly weak and tired.

A dear friend reached out with the opportunity to go to Myrtle Beach for Christmas. They had a place there that they wanted to donate to Virginia. I remember those difficult conversations with Jenn. She was weak, and what if she passed away in S.C.? What if there was an emergency in the car ride down there? How would she get her blood transfusions? Would our car even make it down there? All of these questions were swirling in my mind. I wanted Virginia Rose to see the beach again, she loved the beach.

Virginia Rose and her cousin would go to Myrtle Beach with MiMi. It was a special place, filled with wonderful memories. A final trip there for Christmas would be amazing, but I had so many doubts.

There are times in our lives, when we have doubts, God sends someone to replant our feet and believe. For me, that was Jenn. Jenn, with unwavering confidence, said if God has promised this to her. If HE has taken her this far. He will not fail now. If He wants her to go to Myrtle, He will provide.

Over the next week, all my doubts were resolved. Not just resolved but shattered. MCV reached out and set up a scheduled transfusion for her while down there, and then... as Virginia's story was being picked up around the world, a local non-profit, Mason's Toybox showed up to give Virginia Rose a Christmas party. Her big present, a van! Here they came down our street with presents and gifts and a van. Just what we needed to make the trip to Myrtle Beach. A trip to the beach we had not publicly shared (I was not sure we would even go). In just a few days, God has provided exactly what Virginia Rose would need to go to the beach for Christmas. Jenn was right.

We headed down to Myrtle Beach for Christmas. Our new little van was great. Virginia Rose loved it. So clean, and it even had a movie player for her videos. The villa was all decorated by the staff. They were anticipating our arrival there and even had a little Christmas tree set up in the villa with donated presents under the tree. The front door was decorated, and the lobby had a large Merry Christmas Virginia Rose sign displayed.

As Virginia Rose, Jenn, and the boys got settled into her villa, MiMi and PaPa were just down the road at "Sandy Beach" as Virginia called it, in their camper. She had wanted to go all year, but with treatments and quarantine, couldn't. It was going to be a wonderful Christmas. One that a month ago, we were not sure Virginia Rose would make it to. This was truly God's Christmas gift to Virginia Rose.

She was sleeping a lot more, and her energy level was low, but she had an amazing time. That Christmas morning was so special. As she opened her gifts and played on the beach, wonderful memories were being made.

Christmas morning with Virginia Rose. She made it. God had once again provided and answered our prayers. As we packed up from her amazing trip to the beach, I was reminded of how God was in the big things and the little things. So many times, in life, HE is working in ways we do not even see. Even in the most stressful and painful situations, HE is there to comfort, provide, and love. I am forever thankful for all the angels in disguise HE used to make that Christmas trip possible. All the big things and all the little things.

We got back home on the 26th and Virginia Rose's last trip outside would be the next day. She came to visit me at church on Sunday the 27th, but after a little while, she was not feeling well and headed back home with mommy. That Sunday morning would be her last day out.

When I got home from church, she was resting in the living room with her favorite snacks, watching her favorite movie. The one she saw at St. Jude, the one she scared me with when she fell, "Inside Out". That silly little movie captivated her. She would often use the little stuffed animal characters she had from the movie to express how she would be feeling. If she was sad or angry, joyful, or fearful, she would hold the character. It became a fun little game she had, and after a few minutes, the Joy would always return.

Those next 24 hours she began to get extra tired. I carried her to her room and tucked her into bed. She had a little TV on her wall, and I put her movie on and snuggled with her in bed. By the time she was asleep on December 28th, she would not awaken again.

Those last 24 hours with her were very difficult. We called her nurse and gave her the update. She was so encouraging and loving and was a beautiful angel in disguise when we needed one so bad. I stayed in bed with Virginia Rose the whole time, as her movie played on repeat. We called PaPa to let him know of her change, and MiMi took RJ and Sam back to Williamsburg after they said goodbye to Virginia Rose. We knew the end was near.

On the morning of December 29th ,
PaPa had arrived by her bed, and I was
holding her in my arms. I could feel her
heart beating as she slept in my arms. Then,
just after 9 AM, on December 29th, 2015,
Virginia Rose left my arms and entered the
arms of Christ. As I held her, I felt her little
heart stop and she breathed her last breath.
Her nurse came in and checked her. Virginia
Roses battle was over. No more chemo. No
more meds. No more IV poles and no more

transfusions. She could run again; she could play again. She was free from the shackles and burdens of this broken world, and like a butterfly, she flew.

A piece of me left that day. I know that God has healed my brokenness from her death in so many ways, but there will always be a piece of me gone. One day in Glory, I will get to hug my little girl again. I know it will be a day of rejoicing, and I get to worship my Jesus side by side with my Virginia Rose.

The next few hours were filled with tears and hugs. My dear friend, Wynne, who was there for me and my family during this battle in so many ways was quick to show up. I sat in Virginia's room for a while.

Just rocking in her chair. I still remember his hand as he held mine and prayed. He stayed at the front door, welcoming family for me. The Sheriff's department sent a deputy to stand watch out front, as we all waited for her transport. Her immediate family came over and said their goodbye to Virginia Rose, and we hugged, and we cried. About an hour or so after she passed, I carried her body outside to the car, snuggled in her favorite blanket. I remember placing her body in the van. It was over. Her race was complete. She always was the fast one out of us all.

We followed the van to the funeral home where we began to make her arrangements. How in the world do you plan your 4-year-old daughter's funeral?

It was such a blessing to have Southside and Wynne walking this journey with us. His amazing team took so much of the burden off us and let us grieve and remember sweet Virginia Rose. We are forever thankful for his, and his team's, love and support.

Life After Virginia Rose

Virginia Rose's service was held on January 2nd, just a month before what would have been her 5th birthday. It was a room packed with family, friends, neighbors, and strangers. It was broadcast all around the world and highlighted on the news. The impact of my little girl, the ripple effects of her life, were immediately evident.

Those first two years were very difficult, to say the least. I had my moments of overwhelming grief and moments of joy. At first, it was hard to have joy. You kind of felt guilty for having fun or laughing. I remember the Sunday after her service I was right back at work at church, leading worship. The six months after she passed, I just tried to stay busy with work.

It was about six months after she was gone that the darkness really started to come after me. The pastor I was serving with had left in a bad situation, and I was left alone. Still grieving my little girl and now without my friend who was helping me those six months, I began to fall into a deep hole.

With every passing day, it felt like I was falling deeper and deeper into this hole. I tried to stay focused, and I tried to stay busy. We tried to keep Virginia's foundation going. For those first months, we kept sending out boxes. I remember wanting to keep spreading her love. We sent out thousands of dollars to families, but it was just not the same without her. Nothing was.

By the end of that first year, I was in a real rough spot. The pain and darkness were starting to consume me, and I just wanted to be with Virginia Rose. Everything I saw or heard, would remind me of her. I couldn't go to a grocery store because there was her favorite juice. I kept thinking, what are others seeing. A grown man crying in the kid's juice aisle... I couldn't go to Target because it took me right back to Memphis. Every time I saw a little girl with her family, tears started flowing.

In January of 2017, a year after her passing, God began to break those chains and heal my broken heart. I was leading worship at a church that needed some help for the weekend. Of course, in my mind, I was going to help them out, but God had something far greater in store.

After the music was finished, I went and took a seat in the front. I will never forget that message. The pastor handed us a blank note card and told us to write what it was we had been praying for. I jotted my answer on the card, as the pastor continued his message. He went through a great sermon on trusting God and having a strong prayer life. He then went into a closing illustration that would wreck me.

He talked about how he loved cars and would see one going down the road, and would have to stop himself from getting jealous, or coveting that other person's car. It was a process of self-control he had learned. To be joyful in what he had. We all connected with the illustration, but then his voice changed. It took a more serious turn... he talked about how his cousin had cancer. As soon as he said cancer, I began to get emotional, and angry. Ok, God, I thought, I came here and now I have to hear about cancer. How can you do this to me? He explained how they prayed and prayed for her, and how she went through all the treatments, and this cancer would just not go away. After a while, her body could not fight anymore and she passed away. He spoke of how it was hard for him in those next months seeing someone who was healed of cancer, or who survived cancer. How could God answer their prayer and not his? Why would God let this person live, and not his cousin? I was relating to this sermon and pastor as I had never related in all my years of ministry before. His next word would forever change my life. He said it was the car all over again... there he was, coveting someone else's healing. Being jealous instead of joyful for someone else's answered prayer. That covetousness and jealousy that we were so eager to condemn with the cars, was living out in the healing. By this time, I am weeping. I can only imagine what this pastor was thinking. Who is this worship pastor they sent me? We still have another song to do at the end and another service after this one... get it together man.

After his illustration was over, and as I wiped my tear-drenched face, he told the church to look at their cards. What did we write? What was our prayer? Did it start with "I WANT?" – I looked down at my card, yes, it did. Mine read, "I want my daughter back."

Friends, reader, it was that Sunday morning at Hope Church that God broke the chains I was carrying. This weight, this guilt, this shame, this pain... HE began to set me free. I had dug a hole, in the midst of my brokenness and shame, and I climbed in it. But then Jesus... Jesus didn't throw me a rope to climb out, he got down in the pit, in that dark hole I dug, and he carried me out. That morning, with tears streaming down my face God began to restore the calling and passion He placed on my life. The healing was beginning.

I can still hear Virginia Rose when I close my eyes. I can still feel her warmth and love in so many things. Every day I see her in Samuel's joy. Every day I see her in RJ's compassion. Every day I feel her in Jenn's embrace. Life after Virginia Rose is different, and it has been filled with some hard days, but this I know, she lived a life of love and joy and one day I will hold her again. Her story is never over because her story lives on in so many lives she touched.

Your 9-Months

So, how would you live if you only had nine months to say goodbye? Would you love more? Would you give more?

Virginia Rose taught me and showed me how to live in so many ways. I am forever honored to have been her daddy. She reminded me to live loving others. That even in brokenness, you can help someone else. Maybe that's a lesson you need to hear today. Maybe that's a lesson we all need to hear today. When society and culture is telling you that your happiness is all that matters, when all you need is self-gratification, maybe it is wise to remember that true happiness comes when we love others. That is something Jesus taught us. It is something Virginia Rose reminded us of.

In moments of pain, when the end is near, what will be your final goodbye? Will it be experiences you don't want to miss out on, or will it be people who you impact? What would happen if we started to live like we were dying? Not in the self-pleasure kind of ways, but with genuine compassion and love for others? What if, over these next nine months you looked for ways to be love to others? How much would our outlook change? Instead of being so focused on our pain and brokenness, imagine if we opened our eyes and saw others suffering.

Virginia Rose, in the most difficult circumstances, took her eyes off her situation and focused them on others. She lived to serve others, and love others as Jesus did. Cancer could not steal her joy, because her joy came from Jesus. Cancer could not steal her grace, because that came from Him too.

Dear friends, if there is anything you remember from this little book about a little girl, remember that love, love that comes from Jesus, will sustain you when the whole world is crashing down. That even in your brokenness, Jesus is there. Find your joy in HIM.

Thank you, Virginia Rose, for teaching and reminding us all, it is all about Jesus.

15544004R00069

Stacey vs. Claudia

Other books by
Ann M. Martin

P.S. Longer Letter Later
(written with Paula Danziger)
Leo the Magnificat
Rachel Parker, Kindergarten Show-off
Eleven Kids, One Summer
Ma and Pa Dracula
Yours Turly, Shirley
Ten Kids, No Pets
Slam Book
Just a Summer Romance
Missing Since Monday
With You and Without You
Me and Katie (the Pest)
Stage Fright
Inside Out
Bummer Summer

THE KIDS IN MS. COLMAN'S CLASS series
BABY-SITTERS LITTLE SISTER series
THE BABY-SITTERS CLUB mysteries
THE BABY-SITTERS CLUB series
CALIFORNIA DIARIES series

$$\boxed{\text{Stacey vs. Claudia}}$$

Ann M. Martin

AN
APPLE
PAPERBACK

SCHOLASTIC INC.
New York Toronto London Auckland Sydney
Mexico City New Delhi Hong Kong

The author gratefully acknowledges
Suzanne Weyn
for her help in
preparing this manuscript.

ISBN 0-590-52318-X

12 11 10 9 8 7 6 5 4 3 2 1   9/9 0 1 2 3 4/0

Printed in the U.S.A.   40

First Scholastic printing, September 1999

Chapter 1

"Stacey, Ethan's on the phone!" Mom called from downstairs.

I shut my history book right away. "Thanks!" I shouted as I slid off my bed. "I'm coming."

"American westward expansion" (my weekend reading for a report I'm doing for history class) was putting me to sleep. I would have welcomed any phone call. But one from Ethan was extra welcome.

I hurried down the stairs. "I've got it!" I shouted as I snapped up the cordless phone in the living room.

"Okay," Mom called from the kitchen.

"Hi," I said into the phone. "I'm *so* glad you called. How's your self-portrait coming?"

"I don't know," Ethan replied. "I never thought

staring at my own face could get so boring. I guess I never looked at it this much before."

"Well, you certainly don't have a boring face." Ethan has a gorgeous face. And I'm not just saying that because he's my boyfriend.

He has long dark hair and intense blue eyes. And even though he's an art student, he's also athletic and really fit.

"Well, thanks," he said. I could tell he was blushing. "Staring at myself is making me nuts. Maybe we should have gone Rollerblading in Central Park after all."

I pictured the two of us in New York City, careening down the winding paths on our skates. We'd even talked about rowing on the lake. I could almost see the sun setting around us as we sat side by side on the water.

That *had* been our plan for the weekend before school came along and wrecked it!

Now that it was fall, we were back in the world of homework, reports, and studying. Actually, I like school, especially math, which I happen to be good at. But it was not making things between Ethan and me easy.

He attends a high school of the arts in New York

City (he's fifteen). I'm here in Connecticut, in eighth grade at Stoneybrook Middle School.

I was born in the city, but my parents moved to Stoneybrook when I was in seventh grade. After they got divorced, I decided to live here with Mom, but Dad is in New York again.

I met Ethan while I was baby-sitting for friends of ours in the city. (It was during a school vacation, and I was staying with Dad.) Our friends are artists and Ethan was doing some work for them, helping them set up a gallery exhibition.

Since then, we've been having a long-distance relationship between New York and Stoneybrook. Most of the time I travel to the city by train. That way I see Ethan and Dad on the same weekend.

"Stacey, are you there?" Ethan's voice came over the phone.

"I'm here. I guess I was just daydreaming about how cool it would have been if we'd gone Rollerblading."

"But you had to read up on American westward expansion."

"Don't remind me. And you have to finish the self-portrait by Monday."

Ethan grunted. "The most boring picture I've ever painted."

"I bet it's great," I said. "If you don't want it, I'll take it."

"Sorry, my mother has already claimed it. A face only a mother could love."

"You know that's not true," I said with a laugh. It's a face a whole bunch of girls could love. "Anyway, the weather is still nice. I'll come to the city next weekend and we can Rollerblade on Sunday."

He didn't say anything. It was my turn to wonder if he was still there. "Ethan?" I asked.

"That's the problem. . . ." He spoke slowly, as if he felt weird about what he was going to say.

"What problem?" I settled in on the couch.

"I signed up for a life-drawing course at the Artist's Studio and the only class I could get into is on Sunday afternoons."

"But Ethan, that's the weekend!" I cried.

"I know. I went in to sign up for a Wednesday class, but it was full."

"Don't you take enough art in school?" I demanded.

I didn't want to be angry, but I couldn't help it. He knows the weekends are the only times we can see each other. Why would he take an extra art class then?

"I've already paid," he was telling me. "Can't you spend time with your dad on Sunday?"

"Not next Sunday. I told Dad I'd see him on Saturday so I'd be free to skate with you on Sunday."

"Can't you change your schedule a little?" he asked.

"Can't you?" I shot back angrily. It seemed to me that I was always the one who was juggling my plans to fit Ethan's schedule.

And to fit my dad's busy schedule, for that matter.

I was getting a little sick of it.

"I'll just cancel the whole weekend," I snapped.

"Please don't be so angry," Ethan said. "I didn't think it would be such a big deal to you."

"Well, it is a big deal. I mean, I'm mad because I don't get to see you enough. This summer we didn't see that much of each other. If I didn't want to be with you so much I wouldn't care."

"Listen, how about this? You cancel the weekend in New York and I'll go to Stoneybrook on Saturday. That way you won't have to travel."

I thought for a moment. Truthfully, I was only going to have dinner with Dad on Saturday evening because he had an afternoon business meeting. He's a lawyer for a big corporation and works *a lot.*

I was planning to arrive late in the afternoon, and I'd gotten the feeling that having dinner with me was stressing Dad a little since it meant he'd have to leave his meeting by a certain time. He probably wouldn't mind if I canceled. He might even be relieved.

"Okay," I agreed.

Suddenly, I felt better. I appreciated that Ethan was making the effort to come see me.

"I'll call you tomorrow to say what train I'll be taking."

"Call after six because I have a BSC meeting until then," I told him. (BSC stands for Baby-sitters Club. I'll explain what it is later.)

"Can't," he said. "I'm at the gallery from five until ten tomorrow." Ethan works in an art gallery after school.

"Call Tuesday night, then, but not before nine-thirty because I have a baby-sitting job until then. And don't call after ten, because you know Mom doesn't like me to use the phone when it's late."

He laughed. "All right. I'll call at exactly nine-thirty."

"Nine-forty," I said. "Just in case I'm a little delayed getting home."

"Nine-forty on the dot," he agreed. "Well . . . I'd better go back to staring at my face."

"I wish *I* was staring at it."

"I wish I was staring at yours too," he said. " 'Night."

" 'Bye. Talk to you Tuesday."

"Nine-forty sharp. 'Bye."

With the phone still in my hand, I sank back into the couch. It was true that I felt better, now that Ethan was coming here on Saturday. Still . . . it seemed as though something wasn't right between us.

I couldn't say exactly what it was. He'd been as sweet as ever. But if he were really wild about seeing me, wouldn't he have thought of that before signing up for something on a Sunday?

Maybe I was being too hard on him. I wasn't sure.

I began punching in the number of my best friend, Claudia Kishi, on the phone. Whenever I need to sort something out, I run it past her.

My finger stopped at the sixth number.

How would I explain this to her? It was just this vague feeling — not something I could put into words yet.

I clicked off the phone and laid it beside me. I'd see Claudia in school the next day. Maybe by then I'd have figured out how to express exactly what I thought was going on between Ethan and me.

❋ Chapter 2

I was pretty happy when Monday morning finally came. Going to school meant I'd be distracted from worrying about Ethan. I hadn't been able to think about much else since our phone conversation.

Just before homeroom, I was taking books from my locker when I noticed this *really* cute boy hurrying down the hall. He stood out in the crowded hallway for two reasons.

Reason one was his extreme cuteness. He was tall with sort of shaggy brown hair and huge brown eyes. From the energy in his walk I guessed he might be athletic. But he also had this adorable, lost puppy look.

Which brings me to the second reason he stood out.

I didn't know him.

I can name nearly every kid in the eighth grade,

even if I don't know them well. And I recognize every sixth- and seventh-grader by face.

At least, I'd thought I did. Now I wasn't certain.

The boy walked past my locker and I watched him turn the hallway corner. My friend Mary Anne Spier approached my locker from the other direction. "I saw you staring at that guy," she teased me.

"Isn't he cute?" I replied, turning to her.

She brushed her brown bangs away from her eyes. "I guess. I really didn't look at him."

"Oh, sure," I scoffed, laughing. "You noticed me noticing him, but you didn't bother to look at him because you're so devoted to Logan."

Logan is Mary Anne's steady boyfriend.

"Okay. All right. I saw him. And yes, he's cute," she admitted.

"Extremely cute," I added, shutting my locker.

Mary Anne blushed, which made me smile. She's so sensitive and easily embarrassed.

We began walking together down the hall. "Doesn't it make you feel weird?" Mary Anne asked. "You notice a cute guy but then you think you shouldn't."

"You mean, because you're already going out with someone? I suppose that if you really like the person you're going out with, you wouldn't notice other guys," I said slowly, thinking out loud.

"Really?" Mary Anne sounded worried.

"No, that might not be true. If a guy is cute, he's cute." I was doubting my own theory. "There's no sense saying he's not cute or not noticing. I guess it doesn't mean you care less about Logan or I care less about Ethan."

Mary Anne seemed to cheer up. "That's right. It seems that lately I've been noticing cute guys more than ever before. But it doesn't mean anything about Logan and me."

"Right. Logan and Ethan probably notice other girls."

That thought stopped us completely. We looked at each other unhappily.

"Do they?" Mary Anne asked.

I couldn't answer. The question was too unpleasant to think about.

"No way!" we both said at the same time and continued to class.

By lunchtime I was very hungry, which meant I had to get some food as quickly as possible. I have diabetes. That's a condition that prevents my body from regulating my blood sugar levels properly. I have to eat carefully and give myself insulin injections every day. I can't eat sweets and I have to take care not to get too hungry. I'm sure it sounds like a big pain, but I'm so used to it that I don't mind much.

I was hurrying toward the hot-lunch line when Claudia fell into step with me. "I'm starved," I told her, explaining why I wasn't slowing down.

"Didn't you bring a snack?" she asked.

I usually bring crackers and celery sticks or carrots with me so I don't get this hungry. "I think I left them on the kitchen counter," I said.

"You don't usually forget. Is anything wrong?"

She knows me so well.

I was going to tell her about Ethan when I was suddenly distracted.

I saw that we were about to land at the end of the lunch line right behind the guy I'd seen earlier.

"Is that kid new?" I asked, lowering my voice.

She tossed back her long, silky black hair. "Definitely," she pronounced. "I'm sure he's not a seventh- or eighth-grader, and he looks too old to be in sixth."

Claudia knows the seventh-graders better than I do because she was held back once. She's an artistic genius, super-talented in everything from sculpture to printmaking.

But when it comes to schoolwork . . . not good.

To be honest, she just doesn't care enough to expend much energy on schoolwork. That's why her teachers thought it would be a good idea to put her back for awhile — to let her catch up in the subjects she'd slept through the first time around. She did well and returned to the eighth grade.

Besides that, Claudia has always lived here in Stoneybrook. Unlike me, she went to grammar school with most of the kids. So if she said this cute guy was new, he probably was.

We positioned ourselves behind him. He turned and shot us a shy (adorable) smile.

"Hi," I said. I was about to ask him if he was new, but it occurred to me that if — by some bizarre chance — he wasn't, it might be insulting.

"Hi," he answered. "Um . . . do you know how much the hot lunch costs?"

Dead giveaway. He was new.

"A dollar sixty-five," I informed him. "You're new here, aren't you?"

"Yeah." He smiled uneasily. "I guess it shows, huh?"

"Oh, it's just that we know everyone," Claudia jumped in. "So we knew we didn't know you. That's how we could tell. It's not that it actually shows or anything."

"My name's Jeremy. Rudolph."

I wrinkled my brow without meaning to. Which was it? Jeremy or Rudolph? Claudia wore an equally puzzled expression.

He understood our confusion and laughed. "I mean, that's my full name, Jeremy Rudolph."

For some reason an odd thought flashed into my mind. I wondered what kind of impression Claudia was making on him. After all, not every girl at SMS (short for Stoneybrook Middle School) was wearing bright yellow tights with black stripes under a short tie-dyed jumper and long-sleeved neon-pink T-shirt. Or ankle-high vinyl boots, for that matter.

Not that it made a difference. I was just curious about what he thought. Actually, I was curious about him altogether. He fascinated me. It wasn't only his looks. I felt some strange, unexplainable connection to him.

"Where are you from?" I asked.

"Olympia."

Again, we must have seemed puzzled.

"It's in Washington State," he explained. "At

least that's where we just moved from, but my family has lived all over."

I was more intrigued than ever. I wanted to ask him why they'd moved so much, but as we'd talked, the line had inched forward. Now we were at the front and it was time to get our food.

After we'd made our selections and paid, I noticed Jeremy wandering around the lunchroom with a lost expression on his face. Watching him brought a flash of memory.

I remembered being the new girl in school. Like Jeremy, I hadn't known where to sit in the lunchroom either.

I also recalled the terrible experience of eating alone. You feel as if everyone is watching you and thinking you're pathetic. It looks like you don't have a single friend.

And in the beginning — you don't.

Then Claudia befriended me. She even invited me to sit with her friends at lunch. I felt so grateful and relieved.

It seemed like the thing to do now was to invite Jeremy to sit with my friends and me. (Besides, I didn't want to let him go.) I opened my mouth to speak.

"Why don't you sit with us," Claudia said.

"Yeah," I added quickly. "Our friends and I sit together over there." I pointed to a table where Mary Anne, Kristy Thomas, and Abby Stevenson had already settled in with their lunches.

"If you don't mind sitting with a bunch of girls," Claudia added.

"Why should I mind?" he replied. "Thanks."

Lots of guys *would* have minded — felt dumb or self-conscious. This proved my first impressions were right. Jeremy was different from other guys. Maybe all guys from Olympia were cooler than the ones in Stoneybrook. I didn't know. But I was dying to find out.

We headed for the table. Our friends looked up curiously when they saw us approaching with Jeremy. "Meet Jeremy Rudolph," I said, introducing him. "He's from Olympia."

"Does he know Hercules?" asked Abby, tossing back her mane of dark curls.

"What?" I asked. She's always joking, but I didn't get this one.

"Olympia, Mount Olympus, home of the gods," she explained. "Didn't you see *Hercules*?"

"Embarrass the guy, why don't you?" Kristy said.

"That's okay." Jeremy was smiling. "I know I'm not a Greek god."

(I wasn't as sure about that as he was.)

Kristy leaned across the table and, extending her hand to Jeremy, said, "I'm Kristy. Don't mind my friends. They're acting a little weird today. Mary Anne and I are the only ones who aren't out of our minds."

"Hey, what about me?" I objected.

"You haven't done anything odd . . . yet," she conceded.

"Oh, thanks a lot," I replied.

Jeremy seemed pretty at ease after awhile. He laughed at everyone's jokes and listened intently when one of us told a story.

I wished I knew what he was thinking. What were his impressions of us? Of me?

Jeremy seemed to charge everyone up, to make us talk more and be funnier than usual. But he didn't say much himself. I couldn't tell if he was naturally very quiet or simply unable to find a moment to speak.

It was strange, but I already felt as though I'd known Jeremy for a long time — as if he were an old friend instead of a new one. The only other person I'd ever felt comfortable with so quickly was Claudia. The moment I met her, I knew we'd be friends. I had that same reaction to Jeremy.

He was the first to leave the table. "I have to go see the guidance counselor to find out why I'm in an English class for foreign students," he explained, rolling his eyes.

"Here in Connecticut we think of Washington as a foreign country," Abby said.

He laughed at that. "It seems so far away now that I feel that way too," he told us, smiling. "Thanks for letting me sit with you guys. See you later."

We said good-bye and watched Jeremy leave the cafeteria. "He is too adorable," Claudia remarked when he was out of earshot.

"He'd be perfect for you," Mary Anne said. I sat back in my chair, jolted by Mary Anne's words. Why was Jeremy perfect for Claudia? Why not perfect for me? I'd seen him first. I was the one who was interested in him! Then I remembered — Ethan. Claudia was free to date, I wasn't. Not long ago, Claudia had broken up with her boyfriend, Josh Rocker. Now they were attempting the "just friends" thing and doing better than most kids who try it.

"You saw him first," Claudia said to me.

"I know, but I'm seeing Ethan, remember?" I tried not to sound as disappointed as I felt.

Claudia's face brightened. "That's true," she said.

Then she frowned as a thought occurred to her. "Maybe he's already got a girlfriend, though."

"Yeah . . . back on Mount Olympus," Abby said. "Even if he does have a girlfriend there, those long-distance romances never work."

"Mine is working," I protested.

She shrugged. "Well, most of the time they don't."

"You should ask him out," I said, egging Claudia on.

She sat back in her seat and rubbed her cheek thoughtfully. "Maybe I will. . . . I don't know," she murmured.

I hoped she'd do it.

If I'd been free it's exactly what I would have done.

❀ Chapter 3

That afternoon I arrived at Claudia's house fifteen minutes before our five-thirty BSC meeting. My friends and I meet to take phone calls from babysitting clients every Monday, Wednesday, and Friday afternoon for half an hour. We used to be very strict about this, but now we're more mellow. At the end of the summer, Abby, Logan, and our friend Jessi decided to leave the club to do other things. Kristy, Claudia, Mary Anne, and I — the four remaining members — decided to ease up a little too.

I walked into Claudia's room. She lay stretched out on her bed, working intensely with a pencil and pad. She heard me come in and lifted her head from her sketch. "Who does this look like to you?" she asked, tilting her pad to show me the drawing.

I knelt by the bed and studied it. "Is it . . . Jeremy?" I asked.

She grinned. "Good! You could tell! When you draw a face from memory it doesn't always work."

"This definitely does," I assured her. "Though I think his hair is a little longer in the back."

Claud scrutinized her work. "You're right," she agreed after a moment, then quickly added more hair at the nape.

"I guess you really like him," I said.

"Is it that obvious?"

"You're alone in your room sketching his picture!" I replied.

She laughed. "Oh. Well, you know how I am. I see a new face and I instantly want to draw it. I don't really know him, so I don't know if I *like* like him yet."

I wasn't sure I believed her. If he was on her mind that much then she *like* liked him. (I'd been thinking about him too but, in my case, it didn't matter, since nothing could come of it.)

"How come you're here so early?" she asked.

"No reason." I sat on her bed. "I figured we could hang out a little before everyone got here."

"Cool," she said, still drawing. "Do you want to

go to the movies this weekend?" I was about to reply but she cut me off. "I forgot. You'll be in the city, won't you?"

"No, Ethan signed up for an art class that meets on Sunday afternoons, so I decided not to go. But he's coming here Saturday."

She stopped drawing and looked at me. "Why would he do that?"

"Why shouldn't he? Now I don't have to go to the city — "

"No. Why would he take Sunday art classes? The only time you guys have together is the weekend."

"Tell me about it. I don't know. He had some excuse, like, he thought I could see Dad at that time but Dad's busy a lot too, and it doesn't always work out."

Claudia sighed. "Well . . . I guess he just goofed."

"It does seem strange to you, though, doesn't it?"

"Sort of," Claud admitted. "Definitely. It's strange. Is everything all right between you two?"

"I think so," I said uncertainly. We hadn't had an argument and he was coming up to see me, so I suppose that meant things were fine. But as Claudia and I spoke, that uneasy feeling came over me again.

I suddenly wanted to change the subject.

It was changed for me when Mary Anne arrived.

She was early, since she lives next door now, in the house her family temporarily moved into after their old house was destroyed in a horrendous fire.

"Oh, wow! You did a drawing of Jeremy," she said. "It's great, Claud. We were in class together after lunch. He's nice, isn't he?"

"Really nice," Claudia agreed. "I saw him again on the way to my locker and we talked. He's not all weird around girls like some guys. I like that he's so natural and relaxed."

As she spoke I began wishing I'd been with her when she ran into Jeremy. Why was I so fascinated by him? Maybe I was just looking for something new. Unlike New York City, Stoneybrook isn't exactly a whirlwind of excitement. Something or someone new is a big deal around here. "What did you guys talk about?" I asked.

Before Claudia could reply, Kristy came swinging through the door. "She's baa-aack," she sang out, like the little girl in *Poltergeist.*

"Who's back?" Mary Anne asked.

Kristy took a dramatic pause, then replied, "Rachel Griffin."

Claudia and Mary Anne groaned loudly.

"Who's Rachel Griffin?" I asked. I'd never even heard her name before.

23

"You don't want to know," Kristy replied as she sank into Claudia's director's chair, her usual spot.

"She's like Lucy Van Pelt, Helga Pataki, and Angelica Pickles rolled up into one," Claudia said.

I laughed. It was funny even to think of a person really being like those bossy, crabby cartoon characters. "But there's something oddly lovable about all of them," I pointed out.

"Believe me," Kristy said firmly, "*lovable* is not a word you would use to describe Rachel."

"She moved away from Stoneybrook in fifth grade," Mary Anne explained. She turned to Kristy. "That was three years ago. She might have changed since then."

"Her looks have changed," Kristy admitted. "I saw her in town today when I was shopping with Nannie. She's not a little butterball anymore. Actually, she looks pretty good. Better than you'd have expected her to turn out. But I don't think someone's personality changes that much in three years."

"Did she ever do anything to you guys?" I asked.

"She just existed, that was bad enough," Claudia said. "If you were around her she was in your face telling you what was wrong with you, or what she wanted you to do for her. And it was always something dumb or dangerous. I remember she kept calling me a wimp because I wouldn't climb a certain tree. Day after day — 'Claudia is a wimp.' So, finally, I climbed it and got stuck. She just went home and left me up there. Luckily Janine came along and got Mom and Dad. After that, whenever I saw her on the sidewalk, I'd duck into someone's driveway and hide until she was gone."

The idea of Claudia hiding from this girl made me laugh. "It kind of makes me want to meet her," I said. "Just out of curiosity."

"You *don't* want to meet her," Kristy assured me.

"Wait a minute," I said suddenly. "I think she might live near me. New people moved in two houses down from us this weekend. Mom and I went to say hello and I met the daughter. I think her name is Rachel."

"Poor you," Kristy muttered.

"No," I disagreed. "She seemed very nice. I was even looking for her in school today but I didn't see her."

"*Please* let her go to a private school," Kristy prayed.

The new girl I'd met didn't fit this picture at all. She was pretty, with shoulder-length brown hair and intense blue eyes. She wore a perfectly nice sweater and jeans. There was nothing odd or annoying about her. "I liked her," I insisted.

"Wait," Claudia said. "Once you get to know her, you'll see what we mean."

"People change," Mary Anne reminded them as she sat cross-legged on a corner of Claudia's bed.

"They don't change *that* much," Kristy insisted. "Rachel would have had to change a lot in order to become a normal human being."

The phone rang then and Claudia snapped it up. "Hello, Baby-sitters Club," she answered.

It was one of our regular clients, Mrs. Pike, wanting two sitters for the next night. Claudia told her she'd call her back.

Mary Anne, as club secretary, then looked in our record book, which is where she keeps everyone's schedule. She was the only one free that night.

"What about Logan?" Kristy asked. Even though he'd left the club, I could tell Kristy was hoping — not for the first time — that he'd sub in a pinch.

"Forget Logan," Mary Anne grumbled.

"What do you mean, forget Logan?" I asked.

Mary Anne sighed deeply. "Oh, he annoyed me the last time I talked to him. He was complaining that we call him too much. As if he can't be bothered to take sitting jobs anymore."

"We have been calling him more than usual," Claudia reminded her. "Even though he said he wanted out."

"Did you get into a fight about it?" I asked.

Mary Anne shook her head. "I didn't even realize I was annoyed until later." She shifted position on the bed. "Everything seems off lately," she said. "It's as though somehow the world isn't the way it used to be."

"It's the fire," I told her. "You're in a new house and all."

She shook her head. "It's more than the newness of the house. It's like — if my entire house and all my stuff could just vanish, then . . ." She hesitated.

"Then what?" Claudia prodded gently.

A shiver seemed to run through Mary Anne and she shook slightly. "Then . . . who knows? . . . I don't know." She smiled a tight, uneasy smile. "Who knows what I'm even talking about? It's just a feeling. I can't describe it any more than that."

"It's the shock of the fire," I said again. "Everything will go back to normal again soon."

"I guess you're right."

A weird uneasiness came over me too — as if Mary Anne's indescribable feeling were contagious.

Things were changing fast. Old friends changing and new kids in school. It felt as if people and events were moving all around me.

I didn't like the feeling. If Mary Anne's house could disappear then anything was possible.

❀ Chapter 4

Rachel Griffin transferred into my English class the very next day. I'd heard so much about her I felt as if I already knew her.

Yet the person I saw wasn't the person I'd heard about. I didn't care what my friends had said, Rachel seemed okay.

She listened attentively to the teacher. She smiled when someone said something funny. Her comment about the book we were reading, *The Midwife's Apprentice* by Karen Cushman, was intelligent.

I can say all this about her behavior because I barely took my eyes off her during the class. I was searching for signs of the *other* Rachel Griffin. The horrible one. The one my friends had warned me about.

After class I approached her desk. We were

neighbors, after all. And it didn't hurt to be friendly. (Although my real reason was total curiosity.) "Hi, Rachel," I said. "How's everything going?"

She smiled. "Fine, I guess."

"Do you remember everyone from before you left?" I asked.

Her eyes narrowed warily. "How did you know I used to live here?"

"My friends Kristy, Claudia, and Mary Anne remember you. Do you remember them?"

"Uh-huh."

I couldn't tell if that was a fond *uh-huh* or a not-so-fond one. Her tone didn't give anything away.

"Did Claudia tell you she used to hide from me?" Rachel asked.

"Well — "

Rachel smiled. "She told you. I can tell from your expression. It's okay. Your friends weren't exactly crazy about me."

"I moved away and returned too," I told her. "My family moved to Stoneybrook when my dad was transferred here. Then he was transferred back to New York. While we were in the city my parents split up and I came back to Stoneybrook with Mom."

"I moved from here to the city and back again

too," she said. "Only my city was London. My dad was also transferred."

"London!" I cried. "That is so cool!"

"It was. I loved it. The people, the theater and movies . . . the styles!"

It seemed we had a lot in common. I am a total Broadway fanatic. And I love movies too. And everything about fashion.

Rachel shook her head sadly. "Coming back has been a weird experience."

"I know what you mean," I said. "You don't know if your friends will still be your friends."

"Or if the people who couldn't stand you then still can't stand you," she added.

I hadn't experienced *that* problem. And, again, I didn't know what to say.

The classroom was almost empty and we had to get going before the next period began. "Oh, who cares what other people think, anyway?" I replied. It might have been a dumb thing to say since, of course, most people care, at least a little.

But her expression brightened. "You're right. I'm going to try not to think about it anymore."

"Good idea," I said with a smile. We parted in the hall. It felt like the beginning of a friendship.

For the rest of the afternoon I wondered if I

could convince my friends to give Rachel another try. Especially Claudia. Since she was my very closest friend, I really wanted her to like Rachel.

By the end of the school day I was dying to talk to Claudia about her. I hurried to Claud's locker. But I stopped short before I got there.

Claudia stood at her locker talking to Jeremy. They were having an intense conversation — laughing, nodding, really enjoying themselves. What interesting thing was he telling her?

A flash of disappointment swept over me. It made no sense. Why should I mind if Claudia talked to Jeremy? Sure I liked him. But if I couldn't be involved with him, I should be glad Claudia was getting to know him.

I started walking down the hall toward them, then stopped. Suddenly it didn't seem like the right thing to do. After all, Claudia had been sketching Jeremy's picture. What if she was trying to start up a boyfriend-girlfriend kind of thing? It wouldn't be very best-friend-like of me to barge into the middle of it.

The odd thing was . . . that was exactly what I wanted to do. I had a strong urge to jump smack in between them.

Why?

I didn't know.

As I said, it made no sense. But it was definitely how I *felt*.

Maybe it was that I just liked Jeremy a lot — as a friend. I'd enjoyed meeting him the other day. He was fun and nice. There was no reason I shouldn't have been able to enjoy his friendship, even if Claudia was interested in him.

Still, I knew I should let her have the time alone with him.

It was confusing.

I imagined myself as one of those cartoon characters with an angel on one side and a devil on the other. My angel was saying, *leave*. My devil was saying, *stay*.

I was about to listen to my angel when Claudia spotted me. "Stacey!" she called cheerfully, waving to me.

Happily, I hurried to join them.

"Jeremy was just telling me about this English teacher in his old school who would come to class wearing flowered cutoffs, sandals, and sunglasses," Claudia said, laughing.

"The guy was at least fifty," Jeremy added. "He had this big gray beard and no matter what you asked him he'd say, 'If it's cool with you, man, I dig it.' "

I just knew Jeremy was incapable of dullness. "Did you learn anything in his class?" I asked.

"You know, we did," Jeremy replied. "He gave us the best books to read and then he'd let us sit around and talk about them. It was fun and the other kids had some good stuff to contribute. . . ."

He continued telling his story, but I lost track of what he was saying. For some reason I couldn't stop staring at his face. I noticed he had a dimple in his right cheek. His brown eyes were flecked with green. They were almost like marbles. I'd never seen such unusual eyes.

I thought of the expression *the eyes are the windows of the soul*. It made sense to me now as I looked into Jeremy's amazing eyes. He was different from anyone I'd ever met. Somehow I just knew he was thinking intelligent, insightful thoughts.

"Oh, that's so funny," I heard Claudia remark. She touched my arm, rattling me out of my near trance.

I didn't want to admit I had no idea what he'd just said. "Yeah," I nodded, smiling. "It's funny how some people are."

"That's for sure," Claudia agreed. I glanced at her face. She seemed happy, but not all dreamy-in-love. It wasn't what I'd expected. I've seen her when she has a crush on a guy. She gets mushy and starry-eyed. That wasn't how she looked now.

So maybe Claudia wasn't feeling romantic about Jeremy at all.

It bothered me that this idea made me so happy.

After school I went directly home, had a snack, and got to my homework. I needed to get it done because I had a sitting job that evening. It was for some of our regular clients, the Rodowskys. Those kids are so active that I knew from past experience there was no way I could do homework there.

That night Mr. and Mrs. Rodowsky were home by nine-thirty as they'd promised, and Mr. Rodowsky drove me home. I checked my watch the moment I got in. It was 9:38.

"Mom?" I called.

"In the kitchen," she replied.

Mom was unloading the dishwasher. "Hi, sweetie," she said. "How are you?"

It was the first time I'd seen her since that morning. She wasn't home when I returned from school because she works at Bellair's department store as a buyer, selecting items for the store to sell.

"I'm fine," I replied. "Did Ethan call?"

"No."

Good. I hadn't missed him. I was eager to talk to him. I hoped that this time the strange, awkward thing between us would be gone.

The phone rang. I lunged for the cordless on the kitchen wall. "Hello?"

"Hi, Stace, it's me," Ethan said, recognizing my voice right away, just as I knew his.

"Hi. What's happening?" I asked, wandering out into the dining room.

"Nothing much. I just got in from the gallery. It was really busy. People ask about the paintings and I have to keep finding out all sorts of information, including the prices. Then they leave and don't buy anything."

"I'm not surprised," I commented. The artwork at Ethan's gallery costs hundreds, even thousands of dollars.

"Then why do they ask?" he complained.

"Maybe they're just hoping they can afford it," I suggested.

He sighed. "Maybe."

I waited for him to say something more. I suppose he was waiting for me, because neither of us spoke.

"I can't wait to see you Saturday," I said finally.

He didn't say anything. Warning bells rang in my head.

"You're coming, aren't you?" I asked.

"I need to talk to you about that."

"What?"

"Tonight someone I work with asked me to cover for him this Saturday," Ethan told me. "I had to say okay."

"Why?" I demanded angrily.

"Because he's covered for me twice already." "I couldn't tell him no."

"But you can tell *me* no? His feelings are more important than mine?"

"No way. But it wouldn't have been right for me not to help him when he's already helped me twice," Ethan replied, his voice rising.

"I knew it," I said. I'd wanted to believe he was coming, but, deep down, I hadn't believed it would really happen. I was disappointed and angry, but not shocked.

I was suddenly struck with a terrible thought. Ethan and I sounded just like my mother and father before they divorced. My father was always saying the three of us would do something on the weekend, and then he would cancel because of work. His job was always more important to him.

What a deprssing thought. Was I living a version of my parents' relationship? It seemed like a silly thing for someone my age to feel. Should I be worrying about this kind of stuff at thirteen? I didn't think so.

Deflated, I asked, "What's going on with us?"

"I'm not sure," Ethan answered.

I sunk a notch lower. I'd wanted him to assure me that my worries were silly, that everything was fine.

"It's not going to be easy to see each other this semester," he went on. "I have a heavy course load, I have to work at the gallery, and now this Sunday class."

"So, what are you saying?" I asked slowly.

"Maybe we should cool things down."

Suddenly my chest felt tight.

"Maybe we should," I replied.

I gasped sharply, in a small burst. Had I really meant to say that? Well, I'd said it, hadn't I?

Tears pooled in my eyes.

We both hung on the phone, neither one of us speaking.

"Okay, then," he said sadly after a moment. "I'll be talking to you."

"Wait!" I cried. "Wait. Did we just break up?"

"No," he said quickly. "No. We're just . . . changing things."

A tear rolled down my cheek. I didn't believe his answer. This was a breakup. In my heart I knew it.

"We'll still see each other," he said.

"Okay," I agreed in a choked voice.

"Okay, 'bye," he said.

" 'Bye."

I clicked off and sat just at the table. Mom came in. "Honey!" she said, seeing my eyes. "What happened?"

"Ethan and I broke up," I told her, wiping away another tear. "At least, I'm pretty sure we did."

She sat beside me and took hold of my hand. I wiped my eyes again but no more tears came.

"The horrible part," I began, "is that I don't think this would have happened if we lived closer to each other. I still care about Ethan a lot. And I think he cares about me too. It's just too hard to get together."

Mom looked worried.

"I'll be okay," I told her.

"I think you'll be okay too," she said, giving my hand a squeeze. "You should get to bed. Will you be able to sleep?"

"Yeah," I said, standing up. "Good night."

But I did have a hard time falling asleep. People's faces and their words kept swimming through my mind. I pictured Claudia talking to Jeremy. I saw Rachel. And I heard Ethan's voice on the phone.

But mostly I thought about Jeremy.

✿ Chapter 5

If it hadn't been so late, I would have called Claudia to tell her about Ethan. Instead, I hurried to her locker first thing Wednesday morning.

She wasn't there.

I sat on the floor in front of her locker and tore a piece of paper from my spiral notebook. I wrote:

Hi, Claud —

Guess what? Ethan and I broke up last night. Are you shocked? I was. Sort of. Abby was right about long-distance romances. It's just too hard. I was bummed last night, but I'm better today. Sort of. Write back. S.

I folded the note, stood, and tried to slide it into her locker. Then I pulled it out again. She wouldn't get it until after lunch and I didn't want to wait that long.

This was big news and I wanted to share it with my best friend as soon as possible.

I stuffed the note into my jeans pocket and waited until we saw each other in the hall between homeroom and first period. I passed it to her then.

"What's this?" she asked.

"Read it and you'll see."

She stopped right then and there — in the middle of all the kids rushing past us — and unfolded it.

"Oh, no!" she cried as she read. "Are you all right?"

"I think so," I said.

The hall had quickly become empty as kids disappeared into their classrooms. We couldn't stand there any longer. "I'll write you back," she promised, hurrying down the hall. "Are you really okay?"

I nodded. She was a great friend.

Then Claudia turned and ran back to me. "I almost forgot. I already did write you." She pulled a folded note from inside a book. "Here," she said, handing it to me. "But I'll write you another note about your note."

She ran off again.

I ducked into my classroom and slid into my desk just as our teacher was shutting the front door. The first thing I did was unfold Claudia's note. Then I sank low into my seat to read it.

Claudia is the most horrible speller on earth. But, since I've read a million of her notes, I can understand what she means.

Dear Stacey,

I just now left Jermy at his loker. I like him so much. You were write! Were purfect for each other. Do you think he likes me to? Say yes! Pleeeeeeeese! I hope so. I cant tell tho. Wat do you think? Your hopelesly in love friend, Claudia.

Slowly, I refolded the note.

Claudia liking Jeremy wasn't a surprise.

What *did* surprise me was that her note annoyed me so much.

When was she going to learn to spell, anyway? It suddenly bugged me incredibly that she couldn't spell. How could an eighth-grader still spell like a six-year-old?

What was going on? I'd never cared how she spelled before. I was probably feeling crabby because of Ethan. After all, who wants to hear about a friend being in love when you've just broken up with your boyfriend?

I wanted to talk to her before lunch, but my last class ran long. I didn't get to the lunchroom until all my friends were seated.

And Jeremy was with them.

It's funny how sometimes a thought just pops into your head all at once.

That's what happened to me as I stood on the lunch line, looking over at my friends and Jeremy.

It came to me suddenly.

I had a major crush on Jeremy.

That was why Claudia's note had bothered me. It wasn't her spelling. It was the fact that she liked Jeremy . . . and so did I.

I realized I had lost my appetite. If I hadn't *had* to eat, I'd have left the line and forgotten about lunch. Instead, I moved along in a kind of trance, barely noticing what I was choosing.

If I didn't sit with my friends, everyone would know something was wrong. I had no choice but to join them.

When I reached their table, Claudia smiled at me. "Hi, how *are* you?" she asked. All my friends looked at me with concern. Claudia had obviously told them about Ethan.

"I'm okay," I said.

"What's wrong?" Jeremy asked. (Clearly, he'd been kept out of the loop.)

"Oh, nothing important," I told him.

"Those long-distance things don't work," Kristy

commented. She directed her next remark to Jeremy. "You don't have a girlfriend back in Washington, do you?"

I could have died! She can be so direct — too direct — sometimes.

But he didn't seem to mind the question. "Not anymore," he replied. "We broke up when I found out I had to move."

"See? That was smart," Kristy went on.

"Sometimes things don't work out even when two people live close to each other," Mary Anne added.

"Yeah, but they *never* work out long distance," Kristy insisted.

"I think if you're older and you can drive and take planes and all, you might have a chance," Abby spoke up.

"Maybe," said Kristy. "But not at our age."

This conversation went on for another five minutes but I tuned out. Once again I couldn't take my eyes off Jeremy.

I noticed that he ran his hand through his hair and narrowed those beautiful eyes when someone said something I didn't agree with. I thought that meant he didn't agree either. It proved we were on the same wavelength.

The scraping sound of moving chairs snapped me from my daze. Lunch was ending.

"See you all later," Jeremy said as he stood up, taking his tray with him. Mary Anne, Kristy, and Abby left too.

As I got up from the table, Claudia clutched my arm.

"Stacey, you have to help me," she said, sounding desperate.

"Help you do what?" I asked. (I knew the answer, but I didn't want to hear it.)

"Help make him like me. I can't think of anything else but him."

"But what do you want me to do?"

"Talk to him. Find out what he thinks of me."

"I can't do that."

"Yes, you can. Oh, please, Stacey. You're my best friend. You've got to do this for me. I'm losing my mind."

This was horrible. I couldn't do what she was asking. I was *not* going to do it.

"What do you say?" she asked.

"All right," I agreed.

What else could I say?

❋ Chapter 6

By Thursday morning I'd made an important decision. I'd worried all Wednesday night and I finally knew what I had to do.

I had to choose Claudia over Jeremy.

Claudia had been my best friend for a long while. I'd just met Jeremy. Besides, I had no reason to think Jeremy even liked me. Just because I had a crush on him didn't mean he had one on me.

"Okay, Claudia," I said that morning before class. "You have to get away from your locker now."

"Why?" she asked.

"Doesn't Jeremy come by to talk to you in the morning?"

"Not *every* morning. And I don't know if he actually comes to see me, or if he's just passing by and I'm here so he stops to be friendly."

"Here's my plan," I told her. "If I'm standing here and you're not, Jeremy and I can both wait for you. That will give me a chance to talk to him about you."

She thought about this for a moment. "Should I show up after awhile?"

"No. Because you might arrive before I have a chance to learn anything."

"Okay," she said. "I'll grab my books and go." She pulled what she needed from her locker. "I'll be at Mary Anne's locker if you have anything important to tell me."

"I'll pass you a note if I don't get the chance to come to Mary Anne's — " I cut myself short. I'd spotted Jeremy at the other end of the hall. "Quick, get out of here! Go."

Claudia hurried away from her locker. I leaned against it, trying to appear casual as Jeremy approached.

He noticed me and smiled. (There was that dimple again.)

"Hi, I'm waiting for Claudia," I lied.

He seemed confused. "Didn't I just see her leave her locker?"

Oops. Time to think fast. "Oh, yeah, uh . . . She went to get a book from Mary Anne. She'll be right back."

"I'll wait, then," he said. "I wanted to ask her something."

Did he want to ask her out?

"How do you like Stoneybrook so far?" I asked.

"It's all right. It's kind of strange when you don't even know where the mall is, but I'm used to moving."

"Why have you moved so much?"

"Mom's job. She opens new offices for this big corporation and they keep sending her all over the country."

"How long will you be in Stoneybrook?"

"Who knows? They told her this would be her last transfer. From now on they'll let her fly from one city to another and then come home again. But they've said that before."

I suddenly had a brilliant idea. "If you want to know where the mall is, Claudia and I can show you."

"That would be great," he said. "When?"

"How about tomorrow night? The three of us can be mall rats. We could eat there and see a movie."

"Excellent," he agreed. "I haven't done anything fun since we got here."

"I'll give you Claudia's phone number," I said, ripping a sheet of paper from my notebook. "You can call her and — "

"But I thought she was coming right back."

Double oops.

"I forgot. That's right."

He gazed around at the thinning crowd in the hallway. "It's getting late, though," he observed. "I'd better get to class. We can set it up at lunch, okay?"

"Perfect," I said. "See you then."

The moment he was out of sight, I dashed down the hall to Mary Anne's locker. "IdiditIdiditIdidit!" I squealed to Claud and Mary Anne.

"Did what?" Claudia asked eagerly.

"I got you a date with Jeremy!"

The few kids left in the hall stared at Claudia as she let out a scream.

"What happened?" Mary Anne asked.

As I explained it, Claudia's face fell. "But that's not a date," she objected. "You don't have three people on a date."

"I'm not going to be there," I told her. "At the very last minute I'll feel sick and cancel."

"Oooooohhhh," Mary Anne and Claudia said in unison.

I didn't see how it could fail.

Claudia pressed her lips together thoughtfully.

"What?" I asked.

"I wish he'd asked me out on his own. Then I'd know if he liked me or not," she said.

"After you go to the mall together it will be settled," I assured her. "Besides, he said he had something to ask you. Maybe he planned to ask you out anyway."

"Or maybe he wanted to borrow a pen," Claudia said with a sigh.

"Oh, don't be silly. You've got a date with a guy you really like."

"You're right." She was smiling again. "Thanks, Stacey."

"No problem." That, of course, was a lie. This was a big problem. Talking to Jeremy this morning reminded me how much I liked him. But I was proud of the way I was handling it. It made me feel noble and mature.

I turned to Mary Anne. "I won't see Kristy or Abby before lunch," I told her. "Would you tell them what's going on so they don't jump in and offer to come along too?"

Mary Anne giggled. "I can just picture them doing that and spoiling the whole plan."

"So can I. That's why you have to talk to them ahead of time."

"Okay."

Sure enough, at lunch Jeremy invited everyone else to go to the movies with us. But Mary Anne had done her job. She and Kristy and Abby thanked him but claimed to be busy. Jeremy, Claudia, and I arranged to meet at Claudia's house.

So far, so good.

Claudia phoned me at six-thirty the next night, using the phone in her room. "He just got here, he's downstairs," she said in an urgent whisper, even though he couldn't possibly have heard her. "Do you remember our other number?"

"Of course," I assured her. "Go downstairs and I'll call."

I dialed the Kishis' family line and Claudia picked up. "Hello?"

"It's me," I said. "You know . . . I'm sick . . . I have a terrible headache . . . blah blah blah blah."

"Oh, that's terrible, Stacey," she replied in a voice that sounded phony to me. I hoped Jeremy hadn't noticed. "Are you sure you can't come? Maybe you'll feel better if you take an aspirin or something."

"No, I definitely can't come . . . and so on and so on," I answered.

Claud moved away from the phone. "It's Stacey," I heard her say. "She's not feeling well and can't come."

"Oh, that's too bad," Jeremy replied.

Claudia returned to the line. "I hope you feel better, Stacey. I'll call you when I get home, to see how you're feeling."

"You'd better," I told her. "Have fun."

"Thanks. 'Bye."

So . . . there it was. I'd done my good deed. I'd been the best of best friends. I'd been unselfish and helpful.

How did I feel?

Great!

(I'm lying.)

I felt as if a dead fish were lying in my stomach. Or maybe I felt as if I *were* a dead fish, all droopy and glassy-eyed.

I stood there replaying Jeremy's words — *Oh, that's too bad.* I tried to remember exactly how he'd sounded. Had he been truly disappointed? Or was he only being polite?

Maybe he was surprised, as in, '*Oh*, that's too bad.' Or maybe he didn't believe it. Did his words have a sarcastic edge? 'Oh, that's *too bad*.' Did he suspect he'd been tricked? If he did, what would he think of me?

I worried about that as I wandered into the kitchen and opened the refrigerator, searching for a snack. I tried to hear his voice again in my mind. Maybe he was just being nice. He was thrilled that I wasn't coming.

Then an exciting thought came to me. What if he called later to see how I was feeling?

I'd say I felt much better and we would go on to talk for hours.

But wait . . . I wasn't supposed to want that. Even if Jeremy called, I was supposed to encourage him to like Claudia.

If that's what I had to do, then I didn't want him to call.

Being the best best friend in the world wasn't making me feel nearly as great as I'd expected.

✳ Chapter 7

Claudia didn't call me on Friday night. And I didn't have it in me to call her.

By Saturday morning, though, I was dying to know how the evening had gone.

I phoned Claud at nine-thirty, even though I knew she liked to sleep until ten on the weekends. "Hello?" she answered groggily.

"How was it?" I got right to the point.

"Oh, Stacey, hi," she replied, struggling to come fully awake. "It was great."

Disappointment swept over me, but I fought it back. "Oh, good!" I said cheerily. "Tell me everything."

"Oh, Stacey, he's so wonderful. We ate at Friendly's. I can hardly remember what I ate because we were so busy talking. He's really interesting. Did you know he can speak Spanish and knows Navajo? He lived in New Mexico for awhile. He knows all about the Native American cultures there. He's been to ceremonies and ritual dances and everything."

He certainly did sound interesting. I wished I'd been there.

"What movie did you see?" I asked.

"The new one about the guy and girl who get separated in outer space and have to go through ten dimensions of space and time to find each other again. It was really romantic."

I knew the one she meant. "Did Jeremy like it?" It was an artistic, romantic film, not exactly a guy kind of movie.

"He loved it," she replied.

I should have known that Jeremy would appreciate something sensitive and imaginative — and not be embarrassed to admit it.

Next came the question I really didn't want to ask. But Claudia would know something was wrong if I didn't ask it.

"And . . ." I began. "Did he?"

"What?"

"You know."

"No, he didn't kiss me," she admitted.

I grinned.

"But I think next time he will."

"Did he ask you out again?"

"Not yet. But you know how you can just tell that things went well," she said. "Thank you so much for setting this up, Stacey. You're a genius."

"Of course. I knew that," I joked. "I'm glad you had such a great time."

"We really did," she agreed dreamily.

"You might as well go back to sleep," I said. "Call me when you wake up again."

"Okay."

The front doorbell rang. I clicked off with Claudia and ran to answer it, figuring it was Mom. She goes out jogging on Saturday morning and always forgets to bring her keys with her.

But it was Jeremy.

"Hi!" I said.

He smiled sheepishly. "I was nowhere near the neighborhood, so I thought I'd drop by."

I smiled.

"No . . . really. You were the only McGill in the phone book. And I was wondering how you were feeling," he added.

"Much better," I said — which was suddenly true. "Come on in."

He stepped into the hallway and I led him to the kitchen. Mom's rule is that I can invite a boy in when she's not here if we stay in the kitchen.

Words can't describe how excited I was at that moment. I felt as if I were having a great big happy dream and any minute I might wake up. Until I did, though, I planned to enjoy every second.

Jeremy had come to see how I was feeling.

How sweet was that?!

"Want something to eat or drink?" I offered. "Some soda or juice?"

"No, thanks. I felt bad that you couldn't come last night."

He did?

Wham! My heart slammed into my chest.

"Me too. How'd the date go?"

He wrinkled his brow. "Date?"

Another oops. "I meant . . . you know . . . whatever," I said uneasily.

"It wasn't a date," he said. "Claudia's real nice, but . . ."

Now my heart was racing. What was he trying to say?

"I mean . . ." he struggled on. Whatever he was trying to say wasn't coming to him easily. "You know, don't you?"

I shook my head.

"Claudia's great," he said.

"She is," I agreed.

He looked at me helplessly. I felt that he wanted me to come to his aid in some way, but I was clueless.

"But I was hoping that . . . that . . . *you'd* be there."

Was he really saying what I thought he was saying? What I *hoped* he was saying?

He took a deep breath before he spoke again. "Stacey, would you like to go out sometime — just you and me?"

"What about Claudia?"

"Oh, Claudia's great, but . . . you know . . ."

Now — finally — I got it!

But I didn't know what to do with it.

"What do you say?" he asked.

Good question.

Did he realize how Claudia felt about him? If he didn't, should I tell him?

And would Claudia want to kill me if I went out with him?

I could answer that one. Yes. Definitely.

But he was so cute and I liked him so much. And now I knew he liked me too.

It wasn't fair!

"If you don't want to go out I understand," he said as he began backing up toward the kitchen door.

I panicked.

He thought I wasn't answering because I didn't want to go out.

"I *do* want to go!"

"Great," he said, his face lighting up.

"But I'm not sure I can," I added.

"What's the problem?"

"Well . . . it's not you. And it's not another boyfriend either. But I can't say more than that . . . except I would really love to — if I could. But I don't know."

"Okay, that really clears things up," he joked.

"I'm sorry. Could I call you tomorrow night with an answer?"

"Sure. I didn't mean to upset you or anything."

"No, you haven't. Really. Actually, I'm very glad you asked."

Jeremy smiled and said good-bye, letting himself out the back door.

I sank onto a kitchen chair, still staring at the place where he'd stood.

He liked me. Me!

It was too wonderful to believe.

But it was true. He'd stood right here in this very kitchen and said it. Out loud!

I had *no* idea what I was going to do.

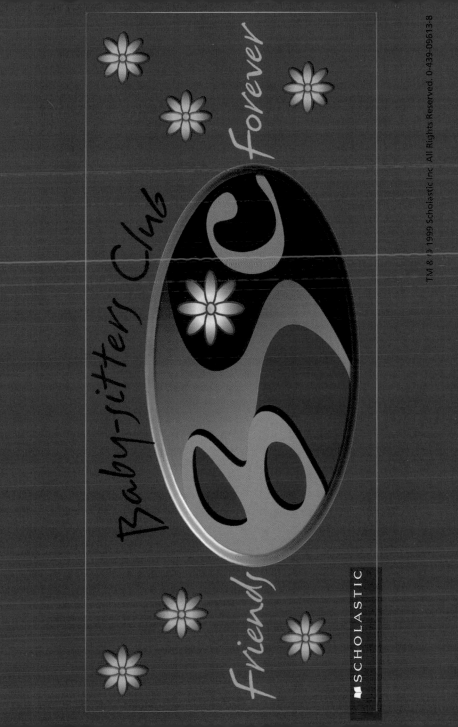

Baby-sitters Club

Forever

Friends

BSC

SCHOLASTIC

❁ Chapter 8

It seemed strange to me that I'd ever thought of myself as the best best friend in the world. Because now I thought of myself as the worst friend anyone could have.

Not that I'd done anything wrong.

Yet.

I was sure considering it, though. If Jeremy wasn't interested in Claudia, anyway . . . then what did it matter if I went out with him?

He wasn't going to ask Claudia for a date.

There was no sense in both of us losing out. Was there?

But would Claudia see it that way?

That was the problem.

I spent the rest of Saturday thinking about this. Worrying. Agonizing.

A true best friend would say, "No way. This is a guy my friend likes. I can't even think about it."

Or would she?

"Stacey, what's wrong?" Mom asked over dinner. "Your head is somewhere else. Is it Ethan?"

Wow! I hadn't even *thought* about him in two days. Maybe I really was the most fickle, heartless person on earth.

"No," I admitted. I decided to tell her everything. "Claudia and I both like the same boy, only he likes me and not her."

"Uh-oh. What are you going to do?"

"I don't know. What *should* I do?"

She thought a moment before speaking. "How much do you like this boy?"

"A lot?"

"And Claudia?"

"A lot."

"Oh, dear."

"Tell me what to do," I pleaded.

"Sorry, hon. I can't. Because I don't know. You should talk to Claudia, though."

I groaned. I couldn't picture telling any of this to Claudia. She'd be so mad at me. I knew she would.

Mom shook her head. "You're in a tough situation."

Like she had to tell me that!

I tried not to think about Claud that night. But in the morning, as soon as I opened my eyes, all my anxious thoughts flooded back. Normally, I would have talked to Claudia about a problem. Or I might have discussed it with Ethan over the weekend. Neither was a choice.

From downstairs I heard the front door close. I knew Mom had gone for her morning run. She says that although she runs for the exercise, it also clears her head and helps her think better.

That's what I needed. Something to clear my head.

I dressed in navy-blue sweats, hurried downstairs, had a muffin and some juice, then went outside.

It was cool, which was nice for jogging. Since it was early on Sunday, not many people were out. I began to run at an easy pace.

I discovered that Mom was right. After about a block I stopped worrying about Claudia. I simply looked at the houses and plants as I passed. I let my mind go blank.

When I turned the corner, I spotted another jogger heading toward me. It was Rachel Griffin. "Hi," she called, slowing down as we neared each other. "I see you're a jogger too."

"I just started this morning," I confessed, stopping.

She jogged lightly in place. "It's not good to stop because your muscles tighten up. Why don't we jog together? I'll turn around and go your way."

"Okay," I agreed. We began jogging side by side. It was nice to have someone to keep pace with.

"Is something the matter?" she asked after half a block.

I turned toward her, surprised. "How did you know?"

She shrugged as she ran. "When kids our age jog, they're either overweight, training, or worried. You're not overweight. Are you training for something?" I shook my head. "Then you're worried."

I slowed to a walk and she did too. "Could we talk?"

"Sure."

I was happy to have someone to discuss this with, someone totally uninvolved. I told her everything.

"Even if you don't go out with him, he's not ask-ing Claudia out. Right?" Rachel asked.

"Right."

"It *would* be sleazy for you to go out with him without talking to her, though," she said thoughtfully.

"But I *can't* talk to her!"

"I think you have to. If she's really a friend, she'll understand. She won't be happy. Her feelings will be hurt. But that's how it goes sometimes."

"She'll think I stole him from her," I objected.

"But you didn't. That's part of what you have to point out to her. Do you think this guy is worth the trouble?"

"I like him a lot," I replied.

"Then if he's worth it . . . he's worth it. If he's not interested in Claudia, and then you turn him down eventually he's going to ask out someone else. Hey, maybe I should go out with him."

"Rachel!" I cried.

She laughed. "Just kidding. But see what I mean? How would you feel if some third person came along and got him?"

"Stupid, I suppose," I answered. "You're good at sorting things out. You're right. If this were a movie, that's how the story would end if my character turned down the Jeremy character."

"I suppose I think in terms of plots, since I'm such a play and movie fan," she said.

"Me too!" I cried. "A total fanatic."

"I want to be an actress. I studied acting in London. Even got a small role in a BBC drama."

I knew, from watching public TV, that BBC meant British Broadcasting Corporation. "You were on TV? How cool!"

"It was really exciting," she said. "I played the daughter of a woman who was murdered. In the story they thought I did it until a private detective proved I was innocent. All I had to do was keep saying, 'I didn't do it. I didn't.' But it was great."

When she said "I didn't do it!" she slipped into a convincing British accent.

"I believed you were a true Brit just then," I commented.

"I wasn't in London long enough to pick up the accent for real, but I've heard it enough to put it on. I wish I had picked it up. A British accent would be so cool."

"It would," I agreed.

We walked back to the block where we'd met. I was feeling pretty good. Talking to Rachel had cheered me up.

"It's easy to talk to you," I told her.

"You too!" she said. Then she gazed up the block. "I'd better get back. Mom wanted me to go with her to the airport. Friends from England are arriving."

"Thanks for listening," I said.

"Anytime," she called over her shoulder as she jogged off. "I mean it."

Unfortunately, my good mood faded quickly after Rachel left.

When I got home, Mom was still out jogging. The message light on our answering machine blinked, so I checked it.

Hi, it's Ethan. Just calling to see how you are. I'll be at my class from noon till two. After that you can reach me at the gallery or at home tonight after eight. Call me, okay? 'Bye.

I wasn't excited to hear from him. Why should I call him? What was the point anymore?

We could *say* we hadn't completely broken up, but we had. Maybe it had been coming for awhile. We hadn't made much time to see each other over the summer. Back then I'd thought it was just bad luck. Now I was starting to realize that when you really care about another person, you make the time for him.

Our relationship had probably started fading months ago and I just hadn't seen it.

I wandered into the living room and threw myself onto the couch.

I'd promised Jeremy an answer by tonight. I couldn't call him, though — not until I talked to Claudia.

Chapter 9

Monday morning came way too soon. After a night of tossing and worrying, I woke up with scratchy, dry eyes. I was dreading what I was about to do.

I pulled off my nightgown and began to get dressed. Then I stopped, remembering something important. I swept a pack of lined index cards from my dresser and put them in the front pocket of my backpack. I had actually written down what I planned to say to Claudia. I figured I might be so nervous that I'd forget.

I felt I'd put together an argument so convincing that Claudia had to see things my way. I was actually pretty proud of myself.

On the first card I'd written:

Claudia, you know that I value your friendship more than anything on earth. I would never do something to hurt you. Your feelings are completely important to me. In this case, though, I'm afraid you will soon learn some disappointing news. This has nothing to do with me.

On card two, I revealed the bad news, that Jeremy didn't like her in *that* way. I used the most gentle words I could think of:

Although he thinks you are a really great person — which is totally true — he doesn't have that romantic feeling. I'm sure he hopes you and he can be close friends.

The third card went on to list her great qualities. I also mentioned that a lot of boys would notice these things about her and would be interested. Jeremy wasn't the only guy in the world, after all.

I knew card three was really just a stall. I felt I'd need that time to work up the nerve for the fourth card.

As you may have guessed, on card four I asked if she'd mind if I went out with Jeremy. Here I took a risk.

I said that if she minded, I wouldn't do it.

I was, of course, counting on her to say she

didn't mind. I'd been very concerned about her feelings. I hoped she'd care about my feelings just as much. She wouldn't want me to be miserable over Jeremy. Would she?

Armed with my well-thought-out, logical cards, I headed for school. I went directly to Claudia's locker.

She was there, putting her books into her locker. I froze.

Was this really the time and place to have this talk — in the middle of the hallway, with kids all around us?

Probably not.

I'd have the chance to speak with her privately after lunch. It was still warm enough to go outside. We'd find a spot alone out there.

I backed down the hall. When I turned, I was face-to-face with Jeremy. "Oh . . . hi," I said, startled to see him. (Was it possible that he'd grown cuter over the weekend?)

"Hi," he said, seeming uncomfortable. "I went out for a little while last night, so I wasn't sure if you called or not."

"Ummmm . . . no . . . I didn't," I admitted. "I'm going to talk to Claudia and see what she says."

"Okay. Whatever you decide. You know . . . But I hope you decide to . . . you know."

"I hope so too," I said.

His entire face lit up. "Okay, see you." He turned and hurried down the hall.

It wasn't fair to keep him hanging like this. I had to talk to Claudia after lunch.

But at lunch, as I walked toward our table, carrying my tray, I saw that Claudia wasn't there.

Neither was Jeremy.

I had a moment of true panic. Had Jeremy decided to talk to Claudia himself?

My heard pounding, I scanned the lunchroom, searching for them.

Then I spotted Jeremy sitting with some guys.

What a relief!

"What's wrong?" Mary Anne asked from behind me.

"Oh, nothing. I was looking for Claudia."

"She went to the art room to finish a sculpture model. I think she's working on a clay model of Jeremy's head."

"Of Jeremy's head?" I gasped.

Mary Anne giggled. "Yeah. He's all she thinks about lately." I followed Mary Anne to our lunch table, feeling sick. Claud was making a sculpture of Jeremy!

After lunch, I worked up my nerve to go to the

art room. Claudia wasn't there. But the clay model of Jeremy's head was.

As I stood looking at it, she came in.

"What do you think?" she asked.

"It's great," I replied honestly.

"It does look like him, doesn't it?" she said, tweaking a clay curl. "It's like his face is burned into my brain."

I had to talk to her. I plunged my hand into my sweater pocket. Empty.

The index cards were in my locker.

To be honest, I was relieved. How could I talk to her with this clay face of Jeremy staring at us?

"It's really good," I said. I felt so hypocritical, standing there admiring her artwork — and all the while preparing to smash her dreams. I needed to get out of there.

"I have to use the girls' room," I lied. " 'Bye." I dashed out as fast as I could.

I really did go into the girls' room, just so I could stand in a stall and be alone. Why did Claudia have to like Jeremy so much? They'd had only one date — and it hadn't even been a date!

When I finally came out of the stall, Rachel was in front of the mirror, fixing her hair. "Hi," she said. "You okay? You look a little freaked."

Either she was very observant, or I really looked bad.

I checked to make sure no one else was in the bathroom. "I tried to talk to Claudia, but she was sculpting a bust of Jeremy. I couldn't," I told her.

"Oh, wow! That *would be* hard."

"But Jeremy is waiting for my answer. I can't leave him hanging forever."

"You definitely have to tell her. When will you see her again?"

"We have a BSC meeting this afternoon. I could go early and talk to her."

Rachel nodded. "That's what you should do."

"I will," I said, filled with new determination.

The bell rang, signaling the end of lunch. As she left the bathroom Rachel wished me good luck.

I'd need it.

That afternoon, I had a special Math Club meeting. A big tournament was coming up and we were planning to enter.

The meeting ended at four-thirty. To my surprise, Claudia came to the classroom just as we were leaving.

"What are you doing here so late?" I asked her.

"I wanted to finish the sculpture. Anything we

need baked in the next kiln firing has to be done by tomorrow morning."

"What are you going to do with it?" I asked as we walked down the hall together.

"Keep it for now. Once I know Jeremy better, maybe I'll give it to him." A frown creased her forehead. "Did Jeremy seem odd to you today?"

"I didn't see much of him," I said. "Why?"

"I saw him in the hall a couple of times and he didn't even stop. He waved, but he just kept going."

"I guess he was in a hurry." I felt like a real rat. I couldn't just come out and say why he was avoiding her, even though I knew perfectly well.

Claudia sighed. "I guess."

She followed me to my locker, where I got my books. I made sure to remember the index cards.

"What are those for?" she asked as I slipped them into my coat pocket.

That might have been the perfect moment to tell her.

"For a vocabulary test," I lied. Once again, I'd chickened out.

We walked home together. All the while I was trying to work up the nerve to talk about Jeremy.

"You're quiet today," Claudia observed when we were almost at her house.

I laughed self-consciously. "Am I?"

"Yeah. Anything the matter?" she asked.

This was it. There would be no better moment than right now.

"Actually . . . yes. There is," I began.

"What?"

"It's about Jeremy."

She gazed at me wide-eyed.

"You see . . . uh . . . It's kind of hard to say this."

A worried expression swept across her face.

I began walking faster. I'm not sure why. Part of me probably wanted to run away.

"What is it, Stacey? Is something wrong with him?"

"You could say that," I replied. "Listen, Claud, we have a problem. Maybe it's a big problem, maybe it's not. It all depends on how you feel about it. I hope it won't be a big problem."

"Just tell me!"

"Okay." I stopped on the sidewalk in front of her house. "Jeremy likes me and wants to go out with me."

There. I'd said it.

Claudia gazed at me blankly, as if she were still waiting for me to tell her my news. As if she hadn't heard what I'd said.

"He likes you as a friend," I went on. "But he asked me on a date. I'd like to go, so I was hoping you wouldn't mind."

I looked at her for a reaction.

Still none.

I remembered the index cards in my coat pocket. If I used those maybe she'd understand better what I was saying.

With a shaking hand, I reached in. But I was so nervous, I dropped them and they spilled to the ground.

"Oops," I said, laughing nervously as I stooped to pick them up.

"How can you laugh?" Claudia cried.

I jerked up to look at her. "Claudia, I . . ."

It was scary. I'd never seen her look so mad.

"Are you serious about this?" she asked angrily.

"Sort of . . . yeah. Definitely." I couldn't back down now.

She turned away from me, then whirled back. "Did he actually ask you out?"

I nodded.

"How can you do this to me, Stacey?"

"I didn't do anything," I insisted. "I can't help it if he doesn't like you in that way."

"You're lying. I don't believe you."

"He told me."

"He was lying to you, then," Claudia insisted. "We had a great time on our date. It doesn't make sense."

"He didn't think of it as a date," I told her. "He really likes you, but as a friend. So that's why it doesn't matter whether I go out with him or someone else does."

This may not have been the best way to say this, but it's what came out.

"I *do* mind if you go out with Jeremy," Claudia informed me. "I *totally* mind. I can't believe you would betray me like this."

"Betray you!" I exclaimed. "Isn't that a bit dramatic? I didn't betray you. I — "

"What's happening?" It was Kristy, arriving in front of Claudia's house for the BSC meeting. She looked puzzled as she glanced from me to Claudia.

"Nothing," Claudia snapped. She turned sharply and stomped into the house ahead of us.

Kristy studied me. "Nothing?"

"We were just having a little argument," I said. There was no sense in dragging everyone else into the mess.

Kristy didn't seem convinced, but maybe she figured it was none of her business. "All right. If you say so."

"Hi," Mary Anne said, joining us. "What's going on?"

"Claudia and Stacey are fighting," Kristy told her.

"Not exactly fighting," I said.

"If you say so," Kristy repeated.

We went into the house and up to Claudia's room. She sat on her bed, stuffing a Ring-Ding into her mouth.

"Are you okay?" Mary Anne asked her.

Claudia swallowed and got off her bed. "I'm fine," she said tensely. She brushed crumbs from the bed so violently that the pillow bounced to the floor.

"Okay, well, since the four of us are here, we might as well start a little early," Kristy suggested, settling into Claudia's director's chair.

Claudia reached under her bed and pulled out a big bag of potato chips. "Here," she said flatly, yanking open the bag.

Claudia usually gets me something healthy to eat. But today she just plopped back onto the bed, arms folded.

I was hungry. And I couldn't fool around about that. But how could I ask Claudia for a healthy snack now?

"What about Stacey?" Mary Anne asked helpfully.

"Oh, fine!" Claudia snapped. She got up and left the room, banging shut the door behind her.

"I hate to tell you this, Stacey," Kristy said, "but she's more than a little mad. What happened?"

I sighed. There was no sense trying to hide this. Kristy and Mary Anne were bound to find out. "It's about Jeremy," I replied, sitting on Claudia's bed. "It turns out that he likes — "

Claudia returned, holding a paper plate of carrots, some dip splashed messily on top of them. "Here," she said, thrusting the plate at me.

The carrots flew onto my lap, dip smearing my clothes. I jumped up. "You did that on purpose!" I accused her.

"I did not. Look what you did to my bed! It's got dip all over it."

"It's not my fault you threw food at me!"

"Oh, no, nothing's your fault. I forgot that. You're never to blame. You can do whatever you like and it doesn't matter."

"It's just dip," Kristy said. "It'll wash out."

Claudia glared at me as she left the room. She returned with a wet towel and began wiping her bed.

I picked up a carrot stick that hadn't hit the floor and bit into it.

"Okay," Kristy said. "Here's some club business

I'd like to discuss. Since there're only four of us now I think we have to coordinate our weekend activities. We can't *all* be unavailable on the weekends at the same time or our clients will stop calling entirely."

"But what can we do?" Mary Anne asked. "Logan's already annoyed that I'm not always available on the weekends. Since we're down to four members it's really been hard."

"Maybe we should assign free-time slots," Kristy suggested. "We could rotate them from week to week and — "

"Stacey can't do that," Claudia cut in. "She'll be needing all her free time since she's stealing everyone's boyfriends."

"That is a lie!" I cried, outraged.

"*What* is going on?" Kristy demanded.

"She's trying to take Jeremy from me!" Claudia cried.

"I'm not! You don't have him anyway!"

"This is bad," Mary Anne muttered, looking as if she wished she were somewhere else.

"Can we talk about this later?" Kristy asked. "Right now I'd like to talk about a rotating weekend schedule."

"Who cares about that when everything in my life is falling apart?" Claudia said.

"Oh, come on," I said. "Your life isn't falling apart."

"It isn't? The boy I'm crazy about couldn't care less about me, and my best friend turns out to be a two-timing back-stabber!"

"Are you both really that crazy about Jeremy?" Mary Anne asked.

"Yes!" we answered together.

We looked at each other fiercely.

"Stacey, I don't want you anywhere near Jeremy," said Claudia.

"Guess what, Claudia," I came back at her. "After the things you've said — I don't really care what you want anymore."

❀ Chapter 10

I don't think I've ever felt as rotten as I did after that BSC meeting. Mention any crummy feeling — anger, guilt, embarrassment, loneliness — and I felt it. All rolled into one horrible knot in my stomach.

That night I couldn't sleep, and I began to cry. Life seemed so hard and unfair. Why should I have to choose between Jeremy and Claudia? Why hadn't Claudia cared about my feelings as much as I cared about hers?

In the morning, my stomach began hurting almost instantly. What would happen today? I was bound to run into Claudia. What would we say to each other?

Would there be more angry words? I hoped not. I couldn't take another fight like the one we'd just had.

At the BSC meeting, we'd sat for almost twenty

minutes, neither of us speaking. It was torture. I was so grateful every time the phone rang. Setting up sitting jobs was a great distraction.

At school I hurried to my locker, looking straight ahead. I didn't want to take the chance of turning left or right and seeing Claudia. As I neared my locker, I smiled.

Jeremy was waiting there for me.

"Hi," I said. "I spoke to Claudia. I told her what you told me."

"And?" he asked eagerly.

"She wasn't very happy."

"So?"

"So . . . I told her I was going to see you. That is . . . if you still want to."

"All right! Definitely I want to."

"Don't tell anyone, though," I added. "Not right away. I wouldn't want Claudia to hear anything about us from other people. It might make it worse."

"That makes sense. How about just hanging out together today after school? Not a date at all."

"That sounds good," I said. "Now that you've seen the mall, would you like to explore downtown Stoneybrook?"

"Sure. Right after school?"

"Okay. Meet me here after last period."

For the rest of the morning I felt as if I were on a seesaw. I thought about Claudia and felt awful. My thoughts shifted to Jeremy and I was overjoyed. Hanging out with him today was going to be awesome.

Then I'd pass Claudia in the hall. And I'd see the hurt, angry expression on her face. Down crashed the seesaw, dropping me on the ground.

By lunch, I really needed a friend to talk to. And I didn't feel right putting Kristy or Mary Anne in the middle. I could talk to Abby, but it wasn't fair to involve her either.

I found myself heading for Rachel's locker. "Ask me how I am," I said as she took out her books.

"How are you?"

"Terrible. And great." I told her everything that had happened since the day before.

"Congratulations," she said. "You did something hard, but it was the right thing."

"Are you sure?"

"Absolutely." I needed to hear someone tell me that with complete confidence. Rachel's words were so welcome.

"Want to eat lunch at our table?" I asked her.

She smiled sadly. "No thanks. I don't think your friends would be too happy about it."

"Don't worry about them. Fifth grade was a long time ago. They need to get to know you all over again."

"They might be ready, but I'm not," Rachel said, shutting her locker. "Getting used to living in Stoneybrook again is kind of hard for me. I don't need to deal with people who don't like me. Just coping with people I don't know is hard enough."

"If you're sure . . ." I said reluctantly.

"I'm sure. For now, anyway." She headed down the hall. "Good luck with . . . you-know-who . . . at lunch."

I sure did-know-who. I was incredibly relieved when she didn't show up. "In the art room again," Mary Anne reported.

"Probably smashing her Jeremy head with a hammer," Kristy added.

I groaned and slid down in my seat.

"She'll get over it," Mary Anne said.

"In a hundred or so years," Abby chimed in. Obviously they'd filled her in on events.

I shot her a Look.

"No, really," Abby said. "She'll be fine by graduation."

"Oh, thanks a lot," I replied.

That afternoon, as promised, Jeremy showed up at my locker right after school.

And so did Claudia.

They headed toward me from opposite directions. For a moment, I seriously considered stepping inside my locker and shutting the door.

I couldn't, though. They'd both already spotted me.

Jeremy arrived first. Following my horrified gaze, he looked down the hall and saw Claudia. "Hi, Claudia," he called cheerfully as if everything were fine.

Claudia froze. Her eyes darted from Jeremy to me. Then she turned and walked away in the direction from which she'd come.

"Nice try," I told Jeremy.

He grimaced. "I feel terrible about hurting her feelings," he said, and I believed him. That's the kind of guy he is. Sensitive and caring.

"Me too," I said. "But I'm mad at her. She didn't have to make this so hard."

"She'll calm down," he said. "Ready?"

Throwing off my worries about Claudia, I smiled at him. "Ready."

We walked downtown. It was one of those beautiful, warm September days that make you remember it's still — technically — summer.

I felt light and happy for the first time in days. "Want to see Bellair's?" I suggested. "It's the biggest department store in town. My mom works there."

"Sure."

We wandered around Bellair's, just looking at things. We watched the TVs in the electronics department. A music video was on. We danced to it right there in the aisle.

In the kitchenware department Jeremy told me about taking a home-and-careers course in his old middle school. "I made a bread with baking soda instead of flour. It was so gross." He laughed. "Mom watched me do it too. She knows less about cooking than I do."

"What does she make for dinner?" I asked.

"Reservations, mostly."

The afternoon went so fast that before I knew it, it was time for dinner. "Want to get something to eat?" he asked.

I had to run upstairs to the offices to ask my

mom for permission. I caught up with her just as she was about to leave. "I don't even know this boy," Mom said.

"He's right outside, calling his parents on the pay phone," I said. "You can meet him right now."

She walked into the hall with me. Jeremy was just getting off the phone. "Dad can pick us up," he said, turning. He smiled at Mom. "Hi, Mrs. McGill. I'm Jeremy Rudolph."

I could tell the introduction went over well with Mom. She seemed to like Jeremy instantly. They talked for a little while and seemed very comfortable.

"All right, kids, have fun," Mom said as she left.

We went to the Rosebud Cafe. It's not too fancy, but it's nice. Talking to Jeremy was so easy. "I'm used to moving all the time," he said after we ordered. "But I don't think Dad ever gets used to it."

"What does he do?" I asked.

"He's a painter. Abstract stuff." My mind flashed on Ethan for a second, another painter. "Sometimes he sells his work, but my mom makes the real money, so we go where her career takes her."

Too soon, Jeremy called his father to pick us up. I spotted him right away. Jeremy and his father looked so alike.

When we arrived at my house, Jeremy walked me

to the door. "I had a great time," he said. My heart leaped. "Want to go out on a real, official date soon?"

"Definitely," I answered without hesitating. " 'Bye."

He backed down the walkway, beaming a smile at me.

I waved and went inside. In the hall, I did a little dance of happiness. *Yes! Yes! Yes!*

This had been great, worth all the trouble.

I felt wonderful, as if I might float to the ceiling from pure happiness.

"That you, Stacey?" Mom called from upstairs.

"I'll be right there," I called back. I couldn't wait to tell her about my afternoon. I charged up the stairs. I was eight steps up when I noticed the blinking light on the answering machine.

I hoped Claudia had called. Maybe she wanted to talk, to tell me she'd calmed down and everything was all right.

I ran downstairs and played the messages.

Message one: *Hi. It's Ethan. Just wanted to say hi.*

Message two: *It's Ethan again. Hey, Stacey, are you mad? I hope not. Call me back.*

I still didn't see the point of calling Ethan back.

Besides, I was disappointed that the messages had been from him . . . and not from Claudia.

❋ Chapter 11

By Wednesday I was deeply disappointed that Claudia hadn't called. Was it unfair of me to expect her to take the first step?

Maybe it was.

Enough time had passed. She'd probably calmed down, at least a little.

Our friendship was too important to let this fight go on any longer. That was what I intended to say as I headed for her locker before homeroom.

But as I neared it, I slowed down. Someone else was there talking to Claudia.

Jeremy.

Hmm. That was interesting. Jeremy was probably telling her what a great person he thought she was. That's what a great guy *he* was. The best.

I turned and went to my homeroom. Jeremy

would make Claudia feel better about things. By the time I spoke to her she'd be ready to hear me. I'd talk to her at lunch.

After homeroom, I hurried to Jeremy's locker, hoping he'd be there. He was.

"Hi," I said cheerfully.

He didn't return the smile. "Hi," he replied, not meeting my eyes. "I'd better get to class. See ya." He rushed away.

"What — " I began, astounded. Was this the same person I'd had such fun with the day before?

Then I remembered how great Claudia thought their time together had been. Was that some strange routine with him — act enthusiastic and then lose interest the next day?

For the rest of the morning I felt very uneasy. I couldn't wait to see Jeremy again, to find out what was going on.

I spotted him at lunchtime, in the hallway outside the cafeteria. This time he hurried to me. "We have to talk," he said seriously, touching my elbow.

I nodded.

"Not here," he said. "Somewhere private."

This was making me nervous. "How about the music room?" I suggested.

"Okay," he said, heading for it.

The music room was empty. I stopped, folded my arms, and steeled my nerves for whatever it was he was about to say.

"Who's Ethan?" Jeremy asked.

Ethan! How did he get into this? I'd never mentioned him.

"I thought we were really honest with each other yesterday when we were talking. You told me about your parents' divorce, about being diabetic," he said, sounding hurt. "How could you forget to tell me you have a boyfriend? If Claudia hadn't mentioned it I'd never have known."

"Claudia!"

"Yes, she told me you're dating some guy in New York."

"*Was* dating!" I exploded. "She knows perfectly well that Ethan and I agreed to cool things down."

"Stacey, I don't just want to be some dating experiment while you're still seeing Ethan."

"You're not!" I protested. "I haven't even been answering his phone calls."

"Which means he's still calling you," Jeremy replied.

"As far as I'm concerned Ethan and I have broken up. I've barely thought of Ethan since I met you."

"That's not what Claudia said."

Claudia again! I could *not* believe what she'd done. "What exactly did she say?"

"She said she felt pretty sure you two would be patching things up soon."

"That's *so* not true! He's taking an art class on the weekends, the only time we can see each other. Does that sound like a good relationship to you?"

"It sounds like you're having a fight over the art class right now. Once the class ends everything will return to the way it was."

"No! It's not like that. It's over."

"Then why didn't you mention him to me?"

"Because *it's over*, in the past," I answered.

Jeremy shook his head doubtfully. "I don't know. It doesn't sound as 'over' as you say. I need to think about it some more."

"There's nothing to think about."

Jeremy edged out the door. "Maybe it's just me, but . . . I'll call you."

He turned and walked away.

I'll call you. That sentence echoed through my head. *I'll call you*.

Did he mean it? Or had he just dumped me before we ever really got started?

It was strange, but the thought of ending things

with Jeremy was much more upsetting than ending things with Ethan had been. Maybe because that had been dying out slowly. But this felt more like a sharp, abrupt break.

And who did I have to thank for it? My former best friend, Ms. Claudia Kishi.

How could she do that? Did she honestly think she'd have a chance with Jeremy if she got me out of the way? Or was this plain old revenge?

I stormed into the lunchroom — on a search-and-destroy mission.

My target?

Claudia Kishi.

✾ Chapter 12

The little witch managed to avoid me for the rest of the day. "Where's Claudia?" I'd demanded of my friends at our lunch table.

They shrugged.

"What are you so mad about?" Kristy asked.

I sat down and launched into my story.

"Maybe she just mentioned Ethan, and Jeremy took it the wrong way," Mary Anne suggested.

"Yeah. Right," I scoffed.

I was too furious to eat more than a few bites of lunch. I headed for the art room, but Claudia wasn't there. I checked her locker and the girls' room.

No luck.

Wherever I was, she wasn't. She had to know that I'd be out to give her a piece of my mind. Obviously she was hiding.

But there was one place where she couldn't get away from me. And that was in her very own house, at our BSC meeting.

That afternoon I had a sitting job for the Rodowsky kids. The boys were cute and funny, and usually I like to sit for them. But today my mind wasn't all there.

All I could do was mentally rehearse the verbal beating I planned to give Claudia.

And, boy, would I ever let her have it.

I had intended to get to Claudia's early and talk to her before the meeting began. Unfortunately, Mrs. Rodowsky was late coming home. I had just enough time to make it to the meeting by five-thirty.

The moment I laid eyes on Claudia I wanted to tear into her. It wasn't fair to Mary Anne and Kristy, though. We'd already ruined one meeting with our fight.

Instead, I glared at her viciously during the meeting.

She returned the Look.

I'm sure Kristy and Mary Anne were incredibly uncomfortable. They had to know something was going on. They did their best to ignore it, though.

"I'd like to get back to the idea of assigning free time on the weekends," Kristy said. "I've made a chart here." She held up a large piece of cardboard with times marked on it.

I was too busy cutting Claudia down with my eyes to pay much attention. As I held her in my gaze, her face seemed to change. I'd once thought she was so pretty. Now it seemed that deceitful small-mindedness was written all over her face, obvious to everyone.

Why hadn't I seen it before?

The phone rang. Dr. Johanssen called wanting a sitter for Charlotte. Mary Anne offered it to me first since Char and I are so close. It was for Friday night. But I didn't care. As far as I knew I might be free every weekend night for a long time.

Thanks to big-mouth Claudia.

The phone rang continually from then on. That was good, since it made the meeting go fast. The faster the better. I couldn't wait to get hold of Claudia.

Finally, six o'clock came. Mary Anne and Kristy left.

But I didn't.

"Why are you still here?" Claudia asked me.

"Because I have something to say to you. How dare you tell Jeremy about Ethan?"

Claudia glowered at me. "Why? Was it a big

secret that you're stringing along two nice guys? Everyone in school knows you're just using Jeremy. Why shouldn't *he*?"

"You are such a jealous liar!" I shouted.

"Jealous? Of you? That's a laugh."

"You know you're jealous. You can't accept the fact that Jeremy doesn't want to go out with you. Well, deal with it, Claudia! Get it through your brainless head that —"

"Brainless!"

"You heard me! What else would you call someone who can't even spell, who was held back a grade?"

"I'd call it better than being some stuck-up creep who acts like she's better than anyone else just because she comes from New York City."

"I do not!" I cried.

"Face it, Stacey — ten million other people live in the city. It's not exactly a claim to fame. Get over yourself."

"I'm not nearly as impressed with myself as you are with yourself. You think you're such a hot artist that it doesn't matter if you're stupid. Well, guess what? Your artwork isn't that great."

"How would you know? You wouldn't recognize a piece of artwork if it hit you over the head."

"Oh, be quiet, Claudia," I said, turning away.

"Why should I?" she came back at me. "After the way you've treated me I have a perfect right to say what I think of you."

"I haven't done anything to you," I protested.

"You let me talk to you about Jeremy, about how I felt. You even said you'd help me get together with him. And all the while you were planning on taking him for yourself."

"That's not how it was. I've told you that."

"But you're a big liar."

"I'm not. But *you're* a big *loser*. What are you going to do? Follow Jeremy around forever and try to break up his romances? Even if you do, it won't matter. He will *never* want to date you."

She surprised me by not replying. My last words seemed to have hit their mark. Tears sprang to her eyes.

"Just forget it," I said. "Let's stop this before we say things we really regret."

She laughed bitterly, a tear falling down her cheek. "It's a little late for that, don't you think?"

She was right.

Way too late.

I walked out of her room feeling numb and empty. The moment I was outside, though, tears gushed from my eyes. I wanted to crawl into a ball and do nothing but cry. I had to get myself home before I could do that.

There weren't too many people on the street. I tried not to think about them as I rushed home, head down.

Mom was coming down the stairs as I pushed open the front door.

"Stacey!" she cried, alarmed. "What happened?"

"Claudia and I had a fight. That's what happened." I pushed past Mom, ran into my room, and slammed the door behind me.

❀ Chapter 13

A fight with your best friend can be more upsetting than a breakup with your boyfriend. I discovered this pretty quickly after my fight with Claudia.

Right away, before school even began, I felt lost. Normally, Claudia would have appeared at my locker. Or I'd have gone to hers.

Of course, I could have gone to see Kristy, Mary Anne, or Abby. I was friendly with other kids at school as well. But they'd know something was weird.

I didn't want to make anyone feel like a second choice.

Then I thought of Rachel. I knew she had no regular morning routine. And it didn't feel awkward to look for her. So I did.

"Hi," she greeted me. I didn't see any surprise in

her expression, just welcome. "How's the romantic triangle?"

She looked especially pretty, I thought. Her brown hair was pulled back into a French braid and she wore a short denim skirt under a soft bright yellow sweater.

"The triangle is smashed to pieces," I reported glumly. "Claudia and I aren't speaking to each other. And Jeremy isn't sure he wants to go out with me anymore."

Rachel grimaced. "Wow. Is he going out with Claudia?"

"Not that I know of. But who knows what she'll pull today."

"What do you mean?"

I told her what Claudia had done. Then I gave her a replay of my fight with her.

"That sounds pretty ugly. Did you really mean everything you said to her?"

I had to think a minute before answering. "Yes and no," I replied.

Rachel laughed. "What does that mean?"

"Well, like when I said she was brainless. It *does* annoy me that she won't bother to spell correctly. I'm not sure why. It's her business. But doesn't it seem to you that by eighth grade a person wouldn't want to present herself as a nitwit every time she writes a sentence?"

"Does it embarrass you?"

"You know, you're right. It does," I said, realizing this for the first time. "Everyone knows we're best friends. So I guess every time she writes something I think it makes me look stupid too."

"It would bother me," Rachel said.

"It would?"

"Yeah."

"But even though I'm bothered by it, I know Claudia isn't brainless. She's actually pretty smart about things she wants to be smart about, like art. That's why I said yes and no."

"Claudia and I never got along, so I really shouldn't say anything," Rachel began as she shut her locker. "But I think telling Jeremy about Ethan was pretty low."

I appreciated her opinion. It's hard to be all alone, wondering if you're seeing things clearly. "It *was* low, wasn't it?" I said.

"Very."

"And she said some pretty nasty things during our fight. She said I'm stuck-up about being from the city. You don't think so, do you?"

She smiled. "How would I know? I'm stuck-up about having lived in London."

I laughed. "No you're not. You don't seem so to me."

"That's because we're alike," Rachel said cheerfully. "Two stuck-up city girls. Hey, we can't help it if we've seen more and done more than some other kids. It's who we are."

I began to wonder about Claudia. She didn't know much about life outside of Stoneybrook. Even Jeremy had lived all around the country.

We began walking down the hall together. "What do you think I should do about Jeremy?" I asked.

"I'm no expert, but I'd give him a little more time, then go talk to him."

"What's there to say?"

"It doesn't matter. If you like him so much, don't let him go without trying."

At lunch I faced another dilemma. I didn't want to have to sit somewhere else. But the idea of sitting with Claudia was sickening.

I dawdled and got to the end of the lunch line so I could observe what was happening. Jeremy was sitting with the same boys he'd sat with the day before. I waited for Claudia to appear.

As I moved along the line, I realized she wasn't even in the lunchroom.

With that thought, I calmed down. I could eat with my friends after all.

Still, I found that I couldn't relax.

"Why are you staring at the lunchroom door?" Abby asked.

"Don't worry. Claudia's absent today," Kristy told me.

Had she made herself sick over this? Or did she want to avoid me so thoroughly that she'd convinced her parents to let her stay home?

"You look really stressed," Mary Anne noted.

"What's going on?" Abby asked.

"You don't want to know," Kristy told her. "You two looked about ready to explode yesterday, Stacey."

"We *did* explode, right after you and Mary Anne left." I told them about the big fight and what had caused it.

Kristy glared at me. "I can't believe the two of you let a boy come between you. I thought you were smarter than that."

I shook my head. "I think it's become more than Jeremy," I said. "I'm really hurt that she would try to wreck things for me. And I'm hurt that she thinks I'd try to steal him away, that I'd betray her like that. What does she really think of me if she can believe those things?"

My friends were silent.

"See what I mean?" I said.

"It still stinks," Kristy said. "Stuff like this shouldn't happen between friends."

When lunch was nearly finished, I looked across the room at Jeremy. I was tempted to talk to him. But I decided to take Rachel's advice and give him some time.

That night I stayed close to the phone, hoping Jeremy might call.

He didn't.

Claudia came to school the next day. I saw her in the hallway talking to one of her seventh-grade friends.

She noticed me. I was sure of it. She looked away and pretended she hadn't, though.

If that was how she wanted to be — *fine*.

Only it wasn't fine. I felt sick. Yesterday I'd been so sure I was right. Now doubts crept in. Was Kristy making sense? Had I started our fight by making Jeremy so important?

Part of me said, *definitely not*. And the other part said, *maybe so*. It was tearing me up.

At lunchtime I ate in an empty classroom, reading an article for my paper on westward expansion in America.

I heard a noise in the hallway. Glancing up, I saw Jeremy walk by the open door with the boys he'd been eating with. Our eyes met. He shot me a quick smile but kept going.

Sighing, I shut my book. Why did I have to like him so much?

I gathered up my books. Now that I'd spotted Jeremy, I wouldn't be able to concentrate. I walked to the door.

And there was Jeremy.

"Hi," he said. "Can we talk?"

"Sure," I agreed, sitting down again. "Listen," I began, "I'm sorry about everything that's happened. Things between Ethan and me are really over." I knew this was true although Ethan may not have known it yet. "I'll respect any decision you make. The thing that's most important to me, though, is that we come out of this at least as friends, because I think you're really great. Even if you want to date Claudia —"

"Hold on." He stopped me. "For once and for all, I don't want to date Claudia. She's the one I want to be friends with. Not you."

"You don't even want to be friends with me?" I whispered.

"Sorry. What I mean is, I don't want to be *just* friends with you. I was wondering if you'd like to go out tomorrow night."

Chapter 14

"The blue . . . yes . . . the blue shirt is perfect," Rachel said late Saturday afternoon. She'd called to see what I was doing. When I told her I was going out with Jeremy later, she offered to come over and help me get ready.

I gazed down at the shirts I'd spread out on my bed. The blue thermal-knit shirt with the row of small white buttons up the front *was* a good choice. It was sporty but not sloppy. It was great with jeans. Perfect for a bowling date.

That's what Jeremy and I had decided to do when he'd called Friday night. We wanted to go mostly to check out the new bowling alley that had opened in Stoneybrook.

At first, I wasn't sure it was a great idea. I'm not a natural bowler. But he said he wasn't either. We agreed not to be embarrassed if all our balls rolled down the gutters.

"Do you have boots?" Rachel asked. "You won't be in bowling shoes the whole time. Wait, though. How tall is Jeremy?"

I knew what she was thinking, because the same thought had crossed my mind. "Boots won't make me taller than he is," I said, digging out a pair of black ankle boots from my closet.

"Good," she said. "Then I think that's what the outfit needs."

It was odd. I would never have had this conversation with Claudia. She wouldn't have worried about how tall or short a person was. And I'd have been too self-conscious to bring it up, knowing she'd think it was silly.

But Rachel and I seemed to think the same way. Thoughts occurred to us at almost the same moment. I felt very comfortable with her.

I felt uncomfortable too. Rachel wasn't Claudia. It seemed to me that Claudia was the one who should have been helping me get ready for a big date, not a friend I'd just met.

"Does Claudia know you're going out with Jeremy tonight?" Rachel asked.

I nodded. "I mentioned it at the BSC meeting yesterday. I had to turn down a sitting job for tonight, so it came up."

"And?"

"You know the saying *if looks could kill*?" I remembered the angry expression on Claudia's face. "Well, if they could kill, I wouldn't be standing here right now."

"But she didn't say anything?"

"No. Then she'd have had to talk to me, which she refuses to do." It hurt just to say these things. But by this point I'd decided it wasn't all my fault. So I wasn't going to back down.

"It's too bad she has to feel that way about it," Rachel commented, picking up a hairbrush from my dresser. She studied me a moment. "What do you think — French braid or loose?"

"French braid," I decided. "Only I can't do it myself."

"Sit down, I'm practically a pro French braider."

Rachel pulled back my hair and began to braid. I loved the result. I finished off with a touch of mascara and some berry-colored lipstick.

"You look awesome," Rachel said.

"Thanks for your help," I replied.

She glanced at my clock. It was four-fifteen. "I'd

better get home. A friend is calling me from London. I don't want to miss his call."

"His?" I teased.

"Yes, but he's just a friend," she told me, grabbing her jacket from the end of my bed. "Boys can be super pains, but they can also make the best friends. Call me tomorrow and tell me how it goes."

"I will. 'Bye," I said as Rachel left.

There I was — all ready, and still an hour to wait before Jeremy came by. To kill time, I took out my math homework, stretched across my bed, and got started on it.

Only five minutes had passed when the bell rang. Mom was out at a baby shower, so I had to answer it.

Had Rachel forgotten something? Was Jeremy early?

I froze in mid-step. Had Claudia come over to tell me off before my date?

If she had, I'd deal with it. After all, I hadn't done anything I felt guilty about.

I swung open the door, ready to face Claudia if I had to.

"Surprise!"

"Ethan!" I gasped. He stood there looking as

gorgeous as ever, with a bouquet of yellow daisies in his hand.

It was terrible.

"What are you doing here?" I asked.

His smile faded. The horrified expression on my face probably wasn't what he'd expected. "I came to see you," he said, stepping into the house. "To surprise you. Can we talk?"

"Yeah, of course," I said, still stunned. Of all the things that might go wrong this evening, this was one I hadn't even thought of. But it could be a total disaster. I checked the hall clock. There was still time before Ethan — I mean *Jeremy* — arrived.

We sat down at the kitchen table. "Stacey, I'm so sorry about what's happened between us," he began. His words sounded a bit rehearsed. I looked for his cue cards. "It's totally my fault. I was just feeling tired and stressed out when I said we should cool things down. It was the stupidest thing I've ever suggested in my life and it's not what I want to . . ."

His voice trailed off and he frowned. "Were you going somewhere?" he asked. I nodded. "A date?"

Again, I nodded. "I figured we could date other people," I reminded him.

"Can you get out of it?"

I shook my head. I didn't want to get out of it.

We sat there looking at each other, neither of us knowing what to say. I felt terrible that Ethan had come all this way for nothing. But Jeremy was the one I wanted to see.

The doorbell rang, breaking the silence.

I panicked. What if it was Jeremy?

"Stay here," I told Ethan sharply.

I ran for the door.

It was Rachel. She held out a pair of dangly blue-and-silver earrings. "I can't stay, but I wanted to lend you these," she said.

I heard Ethan come out of the kitchen. "Stacey, I'm not hiding in here," he said crossly. He stopped when he saw Rachel. I guess he'd been ready to meet my date. The steam seemed to go out of him. "Hi," he said.

"Hi," Rachel replied as her eyes darted to mine. "I'd better go," she said. "Remember, Stacey, you have a five o'clock appointment."

"I know. Thanks for the earrings."

She left, mouthing the words *good luck*.

Rachel was barely out the door when Mom came in. "Hello, Ethan," she said. "Stacey, you didn't tell me Ethan was coming."

"She didn't know," Ethan explained glumly. "It was sort of a surprise."

But Mom knew I had a date with Jeremy. "Can I speak to you a moment?" she asked me. "Excuse us, Ethan."

We went to the kitchen. "Mom, what am I going to do?" I said urgently.

"I don't know. Which one do you want to see?"

"Jeremy," I answered without a moment's thought.

"Then you'd better talk to Ethan right away. I'll be here in the kitchen if you need me."

I knew she was right. I hurried back to Ethan.

"I'm sorry, Stacey," he said. "This is *so* my fault. I feel like a jerk."

"Don't feel that way. I'm sorry I haven't been calling you back. I didn't know what to say. I think the problem between us is the miles."

"It's harder than I thought it would be," he agreed. "But I don't want to break up."

"I don't see how we can go on."

"You mean, you don't want to see me anymore? At all?"

"It's just not working. Would it be all right if we saw each other as friends?"

He turned away from me. "No," he said in a choked voice. Then he turned back. "Maybe. I'm not sure. Can I think about it?"

"Sure," I said. Tears welled up in my eyes but I fought them back. Ethan had meant so much to me. But that deep feeling was gone and there was no sense in pretending.

"I'd better go," he said.

"Do you need a ride to the train station?" I asked.

"No. That's okay."

"All right. If you're sure."

"I'm sure." He stepped toward me and we hugged, squeezing each other tightly. Once he let go, he was out the door in a flash.

I felt both sorrow and relief. It's hard to break off something that had once been so meaningful. But I was glad we weren't on that foggy middle ground anymore. Now we knew for sure where we stood.

I went up the stairs to my room. In the mirror I saw that my tears had caused my mascara to smudge under my eyes. As I blotted it with a tissue, the doorbell rang again.

Stepping into the hallway, I heard Mom open the door.

❋ Chapter 15

"Stacey, it's Jeremy," Mom called up the stairs.

He was early, but who cared? I ran back to my room for a last mascara blot. I'd slipped Rachel's earrings into my jeans pocket. I fished them out and put them on. She'd been right. They were perfect.

As I ran down the stairs, I saw Jeremy standing at the bottom. He wore an open-collared blue denim shirt over a bright white T-shirt. His black jeans were neat. His hair was slightly fluffier than usual, like he'd just washed it for our date. Adorable.

"Sorry I'm early," he said.

"No problem," I replied brightly.

"My neighbor told me that if you get to Bowled Over early you're more likely to get a lane right away," he explained.

"You're talking about the new bowling alley?" Mom asked as she walked in from the kitchen.

"Yeah. I've heard it's great," Jeremy replied. "There's a restaurant there that actually serves decent food."

"Sounds fun," Mom said. "Want a ride?"

"We can walk," I replied as I pulled on my jacket.

When we were outside, I smiled at Jeremy. "I'm really looking forward to this," I said.

"Me too," he replied. He took my hand and we set off together.

That night I bowled terribly. So did Jeremy. I think we had a combined score of sixty on our first game.

But I've never laughed so much in my life. We were both so awful it was funny. By the time we sat down in the Bowled Over restaurant, my sides hurt from laughing.

The food was great. And we talked together so easily. Just as Claudia had told me, he knew a lot about Native American rituals because he'd lived out West. He talked to me about how he admired the oneness with nature that they had built into their culture.

He said lots of things that interested me and made me think. I suppose you didn't have to go to New York City to discover new and interesting people and things.

Maybe Claudia had been right (at least a little) about my being a New York snob. I'd try to be more aware of it.

Jeremy's father drove us home. When we reached my front door. Jeremy put his arm around me and we kissed.

When the kiss ended, I smiled at him. "I had a great time," I said.

"So did I."

"Do you feel like doing something tomorrow?"

"Sure. Call me in the morning."

I went inside feeling light and happy. Much too excited to go to bed. I did a half twirl into the living room and picked up the phone. I had to tell Claudia all about the evening.

I couldn't, though.

And somehow I didn't feel like telling anyone else.

When would I be able to confide in Claudia again? Would I even speak to her again?

I hoped so. But I wasn't sure.

I guess I'd been right about all the changes in the air. So much was different now. My relationships with Claudia, with Ethan, now with Jeremy.

I suppose that's how life is. It's a good thing we can't see around corners.

About the Author

ANN MATTHEWS MARTIN was born on August 12, 1955. She grew up in Princeton, NJ, with her parents and her younger sister, Jane.

Although Ann used to be a teacher and then an editor of children's books, she's now a full-time writer. She gets ideas for her books from many different places. Some are based on personal experiences. Others are based on childhood memories and feelings. Many are written about contemporary problems or events.

All of Ann's characters, even the members of the Baby-sitters Club, are made up. (So is Stoneybrook.) But many of her characters are based on real people. Sometimes Ann names her characters after people she knows; other times she chooses names she likes.

In addition to the Baby-sitters Club books, Ann Martin has written many other books for children. Her favorite is *Ten Kids, No Pets* because she loves big families and she loves animals. Her favorite BSC book is *Kristy's Big Day.* (Kristy is her favorite baby-sitter.)

Ann M. Martin now lives in New York with her cats, Gussie, Woody, and Willy, and her dog, Sadie. Her hobbies are reading, sewing, and needlework — especially making clothes for children.

Look for #3

MARY ANNE'S BIG BREAKUP

"Logan," I repeated, mixing his name with an unhappy sigh.

Everyone turned and stared at me.

"What?" I asked, surprised by the sudden attention.

"The way you just said *Logan*," Stacey explained.

"It was the same way a person might say the word *liver*," Kristy put in.

"Or *homework*," added Claudia.

"What's the matter?" Kristy asked.

I sighed again. "It's just that . . ." My voice trailed off. It was so hard to put this into words. "Things don't seem to be . . . the way they were."

"In what way?" Stacey asked.

"I don't know. I used to feel so happy when I

knew Logan was coming over or that I'd see him in school. Now I just feel like — *Is he here again?*" I couldn't believe I was really saying these things. But they were true.

"Things went flat like that for Josh and me," Claudia said, talking about her ex-boyfriend.

"But you and Josh have stayed friends," I replied. "I wonder if Logan and I could."

"Hold on!" Kristy cried, leaning way forward in her chair. "What do you mean 'If Logan and I could'? You're not actually thinking of breaking up with Logan, are you?"

It was weird. Up until that very moment I hadn't wanted to think beyond the fact that things weren't working. So the words that came out of my mouth next surprised even me.

"Yes," I said. "I think I am."

My friends stared at me as if they couldn't believe what they'd heard.